Praise for Dinky: The Nurse Mare's Foal

Marta Moran Bishop has lovingly created the real-life poignant tale of, *Dinky, The Nurse Mare's Foal*. Narrated by the central character, Dinky, readers will be given a window into the heartbreaking life that can await a Nurse Mare Foal's. It is a powerful story highlighting the inhumane practice of a foal being bred for the sole purpose of producing milk in the mare, so she can nourish a high-dollar mare's foal.

Young Dinky's battle to survive begins, when he is taken to a farm where the probability of being sold to the meat market or the tanners, so his hide could be used for leather goods is high. Dinky is frightened and alone. His only chance to be free to live and enjoy life is to be adopted by some caring humans.

Dinky: The Nurse Mare's Foal is an immensely satisfying book which evokes our senses and touches us deeply.

Stuart Ross McCallum, author of *Beyond My Control: One Man's Struggle with Epilepsy, Seizure, Surgery, and Beyond.*

Katmoran Publications ®

www.katmoranpublications.com

ISBM: 978-0-9840051-0-9

Cover Design Charles M. Roth
cmrdesignca@gmail.com
Photo Artwork Robbie Kaye
http://www.robbiekaye.com

Katmoran Publications ® 2013
Bolton, MA 01740

Although based on true events this book is fiction.

This is the story of Dinky.

KATMORAN PUBLICATIONS

DINKY: THE NURSE MARE'S FOAL

Marta Moran Bishop has worked at a variety of careers before taking up writing full time. To date she has three other books available.

Her first two books are poetry. The highly acclaimed Wee Three: A Child's World and her adult poetry book, A Poet's Journey: Emotions. Ms. Bishop's third book is the social cautionary tale The Between Times.

She lives with her husband, three horses, and four cats on a small farm in Massachusetts.

An Introduction to a Nurse Mare Foal

The elite of the horse world are the high-dollar mares. They are show animals or racing animals, bringing high dollars for their foals because they have a history of excellence and winning. For them, time is money and it's important that the mare be kept busy birthing instead of spending weeks nursing her offspring. That job is given to a nurse mare.

Much like the old-time wet nurse employed by wealthy mothers throughout history, the nurse mare is of uncertain or unimportant bloodlines and incapable of bringing substantial income to her owner. In order to nurse the important foal, she must have recently given birth and produce the necessary milk. The question is: What becomes of the nurse mare's foal?

By many called a "junk foal," this unfortunate newborn is considered a necessary evil, a disposable byproduct. The cost of trying to nurse this foal until it is weaned is high, so often the "junk foal" is killed outright and disposed of. Sometimes it's shipped off to auction and bought by manufacturers who use its hide to make expensive bags or shoes. Whatever its fate, the nurse mare's foal is considered an unimportant nuisance.

Introduction

The nurse mare's foal is usually taken from its mother anytime from one day to a week after birth instead of the ten to twelve weeks that foals commonly nurse. The times vary, depending on when the high-dollar mare foals. Generally the nurse mare is shipped off to the farm to nurture and foster the high-priced foal.

The horse industry benefits from this barbaric practice because the high-dollar mare gets back in shape more quickly, so she can show well and invite more offers for her offspring. While some stables allow the mare three to four weeks to recuperate after giving birth, many are sent to the stallion for rebreeding within seven to ten days of giving birth.

There are Equine Rescue Leagues that have spent their time, energy, and money to help the rejected foals. Without them, more of these small lives would be lost. Most of the rescuers are knowledgeable, but there are a few well-intentioned people who want to save the newborns without any knowledge of horses. In some cases these organizations succeed almost by accident, and in others they make matters worse for the animals in their care. Unfortunately these groups sometimes rely on unscrupulous people, self-proclaimed experts who have their own hidden agendas.

Introduction

The lucky foal is adopted by people who know and love horses or who go out of their way to learn the needs and care of this fragile baby animal. Too many are adopted by men and women who know little or nothing about horses, let alone the unique care these foals require, and the new owners soon become overwhelmed. As a result, some foals are bought and sold several times before they reach maturity. Others die from lack of proper nutrition and proper parasite control. The nurse mare's foal unfortunate enough to fall into the wrong hands usually grows up with multiple deformities and bone development problems. Some have social development issues, never learning how to be a horse or understanding the role of a horse with a human companion.

This book is the story of one nurse mare's foal and its fight for survival.

Marta Moran Bishop and Toni Boyle

When we first met Dinky, he was underfed, full of parasites, and so thin it would break your heart. As a result of this, he appeared two months younger than his real age.

Many of the events of this book are true. They were written from watching our horses and in particular Dinky as he struggled to learn to be a horse and understand the world he lives in. The earliest part of the book is based on research into nurse mare foals and my imagination.

Dinky, his brother Chrome, and sister Connella have formed a strong family/herd bond. You can see them grooming each other, playing, and romping together up and down the field.

This book was inspired by Dinky and the entire practice of nurse mare foals.

Acknowledgements

I would like to thank Kris Koss, the very best veterinarian a horse or a horse lover could ever have; Bob Rotti, our farrier, whose knowledge and friendship has been invaluable; Terry Theirren and Becky Ballin, to whom we owe a debt of gratitude for their friendship, knowledge of horses, and patience with us as we learned.

A special thank you to my friends Lisette Brodey, Lisa McCallum, and Franki deMerle, whose love of Dinky's story was invaluable to me. To Robert W. Walker whose expertise and recommendations helped me to write a better story.

Thank you Robbie Kaye, for your work on the photo of Dinky for the cover and Charles Roth who did the cover design; to Toni Boyle, who helped me write an introduction on nurse mare foals and to last, but not least Stuart Ross McCallum for his lovely review for the back cover.

This book is dedicated to Dinky,

Chrome, and Connella.

Dinky

The Nurse Mare's Foal

Marta Moran Bishop

Contents

One

Space

Follow all your memories
They will help you understand
Space is a requirement
To show respect for others

I don't want to remember when I first heard the term nurse mare's foal or who called me Dinky first. I had another name once, but only for a short time. I don't like to think about those times. When I do, I become frightened and angry. I would be so much happier today if I just could enjoy the moment as Chrome and Connella are doing. Unfortunately for me, I'm not in the mood to nap. Today I'm terrified of sleep for fear the dreams will come back. It's much better standing here in the middle of the field, letting the cool, gentle breeze flow through my mane, and feeling the warm sun on my back.

My black coat is beginning to turn white like Chrome's, and I know my tail looks stunning with its

1

multi-layers of colors swishing in the breeze. It is changing colors in layers from the bottom up. Soon it will be entirely gold, just as Chrome's tail is.

I love to stand and watch the ever changing forest behind our field. Winter is still upon us, the trees are bare of leaves, and the snow is gone from the ground. Spring will be here soon. The days are growing longer giving us more time to play. Soon Marta and Ken will be spending more time outside, either with us or sitting at the table talking and watching us play.

Sometimes they will come and play with us, and at other times we will go over to the fence, watch them, and listen to their conversation. Connella said this year my lessons won't be baby lessons but ones for an adult horse. When I asked her what she meant by that, she just told me to wait and see. I hate it when others drop hints about things that will happen and then make me wait. I don't like waiting.

Today didn't start off well. Marta became annoyed with me quite early. Usually she's exceptionally polite about everything; she's even patient with Connella when she takes her time about going into her room for breakfast. It's Connella's way to make us all wait a bit. She pretends to ignore everyone as she looks at this and that, stops to smell a piece of rock, a pile of manure, or looks over the fence at the road or the forest beyond us. Whatever she can do to manipulate us all into waiting, she will do it. She especially likes to prove to me that she's next in line after Chrome. Often she puts her ears back and chases me away if I try to go before her or if I stand too close to her.

It seems that every day someone tells me it's time for me to learn something new. Why can't they be clearer? Why is it so hard for me to grasp some of the things Chrome and Connella find so easy to understand? At meal times, even if Chrome and I stand at the fence waiting when it's time to go into our rooms, Connella makes sure she puts me in my place. Then it's Chrome with Connella standing behind him, and I don't quite know what to do. Am I supposed to go behind Connella? If this is the case, why must it be this way? Both of them have told me it's about learning my place in the herd. In the field, we all eat our hay together; there's plenty of food for everyone, so no one gets pushed aside. What is it about going into the barn for our grain that's different?

This morning began the same, except my new halter had a loose flap. Marta came over to fix it. She scolded

Connella earlier for riling me up, which usually meant that I had to stay out of her way until she was willing to talk to me. Connella gets extremely annoyed if I get any attention, unless she has hers first.

It's odd, because if it's time for a cookie, Connella usually hangs back behind Chrome and me until Marta calls her. If Marta says, "Connella, get with your family," Connella will come up and stand with us, but if she says "Connella come on. Its cookie time," she goes into her room and waits, hanging her head out the window to get her cookie. It's fitting that her room is so close to the gate or Marta wouldn't be able to reach her.

Yet when it comes to meals, it changes; I'm unsure what makes meals different. I've tried talking to Connella and Chrome about it. They both say the same thing, "That's the way of things. You'll learn."

Well, back to what happened that caused today to be different. As I said, the flap on my halter was loose. Marta stood on my left fixing it, when Connella put her ears back and came toward me. I jumped toward Marta, and she fell. It was then that the day went from bad to worse.

After breakfast I tried to help Marta clean the stalls, but she didn't like it; she got annoyed with me and shut me in one of the stalls. Today instead of talking to me, she decided to lecture me while she cleaned the stalls. "Dinky, today you must learn about space. It's a part of learning respect for others," she said to me as I stood locked in my room waiting to be let out. "We all love you, even Connella, who it appears is the only one you always listen to. She forces you to understand and show her respect when she wants space. When you crowd others when they don't want it, and you get too close to them, you're disrespecting them." As she finished cleaning Chrome's stall she continued. (I wanted to go out in the field, but I knew she wouldn't let me until she was finished.)

"Dinky, until you learn to listen to me and not tip over the wheel barrow full of manure, you must stay in your room." So I was stuck, a captive audience, as she continued to lecture me. "It can also become risky if you do it when Ken or I are walking you on the lead rope or you jump toward me as you did earlier. We're going to begin your lessons immediately. Both yesterday and today could have been extremely dangerous, Dinky."

I didn't like the sound of any of this and was getting really antsy to go out and finish my breakfast. Still she went on, "Chrome and Connella took their halters easily.

On the other hand, you thought you knew what was coming and didn't wait for your halter. It's not acceptable for you to push through everybody the way you did last night. I don't care if you think I'm going to let you all into the round pen and allow you all to run and jump with no one in control. It's about time you learned differently. You're a big boy now and it's time you learn some manners. If you don't, someday someone will get hurt. It might be Ken, Chrome, Connella, me, or you. So today we will begin the first of many lessons. You'll learn appropriate behavior about space. I will not have you be a threat to yourself or others."

I stood there looking at her with my cutest little boy expression, but it was of no help. Today it didn't matter how sweet I appeared. There would be no stopping her.

Still feeling ashamed of myself after being chastised in front of everyone, the lessons began. She made me stand away from her; if I tried to come near her before she called me, she pushed me away. Then we had the move over exercises. Sometimes I only had to move my hind quarters and sometimes all of me. Until she decided when, I couldn't come close or cuddle. The big "NO" apparently is if I try to push at her or go first. It was awful, especially when she said, "Dinky, we'll do this lesson a lot over the coming weeks." After she left, Chrome nipped me when I tried to get him to play. "I'm not in the mood right now. Dinky, give me some space."

Still I persisted. I had to have some answers, and so before Chrome went to take his nap, I asked him, "Chrome, why is it so hard for me to learn these things?"

He said, "I think it's because you didn't have other horses around you or a mom to teach you these things when you were young, Dinky. If you had the proper weaning it wouldn't be so hard. When I grew up, my mother began my weaning by pushing me away."

"What's weaning, Chrome?"

"It's when the time comes for you to eat adult food and not drink your mother's milk anymore."

"I stopped drinking my mother's milk months ago, Chrome. Was that weaning?" I asked.

"Not really, Dinky. It was much too early for you to leave your mom. You should have spent about six months with her, and then you would have been moved in with the other foals but kept close enough to your mother. Your mother and other adult horses should still have been near enough to protect and teach you. It's a long process—one you didn't learn, my friend. It's what teaches you about space."

"Chrome, if I never had those things you're describing, how will I learn it all now? I don't like being confused half the time. And I don't like being scolded, though sometimes it's fun to get Connella riled up," I replied.

"I'm not quite sure, Dinky. I know you don't like to think about the past, but I think you might have to. Even when you first came here, you didn't talk about it, not even when Connella and I asked you questions. I honestly believe you'll have to think about those times if you're going to move forward. And you should talk about them too."

"You don't understand, Chrome. It's so scary to remember, and I feel so terrified—almost as if the darkness will kill me."

"Still, I think you must face your fears, Dinky. Then you'll be able to understand things easier."

I didn't like the tone the conversation was taking, so I walked off thinking. Maybe space meant I could only get close to someone when I was invited. I didn't like that either. Why should I have to be the one to lose out on what I needed? Chrome told me that it was only a matter of time, and then I'd feel happy about my place. I would have to earn it. Lessons were hard work, and I wasn't quite sure I liked them.

I was still unsure what the difference was between a lesson and play. But I did know that the lessons about space weren't my favorite. In fact, I was sure I didn't like them at all. They reminded me of some of the bad times. Oh, I didn't want to think about the bad times. I hated to ruminate on those dark, scary, lonely times. I was afraid. I knew today the memories would come, what with Chrome and Connella napping and me standing here thinking about today's lesson and what it all meant.

Don't get me wrong, most days here were terrific. I felt loved and wanted. Sometimes the memories were wonderful ones, and I laughed and felt happy. Then there were days like today when I got reprimanded. It was then that I started recalling things and the darkness came alive. Usually I could find something to distract me or a game to play. I was afraid today I might not be as successful. The lesson on space made me feel alone, small, and helpless again. As the memories washed over me, I felt myself going down a long black tunnel. The sunlight had vanished. The familiar forest behind our

9

field was gone. I was alone in my mind in the dark again.

Two

Mother

Curiosity first
Then the bubble will burst
Loss and sorrow follows
Before next day's cock crows

Wet and shivering I lay on the ground, my mother and I still connected. She was murmuring sweet things in my ears, filling my mind and heart with her love as she cleaned the blood and birthing fluids off of me. Overhead the stars and moon hung low in the sky. The wisps of clouds were thickening. The love I felt was so deep and strong, yet this new world was beginning to call me now.

"Son, you must stand now," she said. "It is time, and you need to eat." With the light of the full moon, her white coat was glowing. She nudged me again to stand. The first few times I fell, my young legs wobbly and not used to bearing my weight. "Good boy."

Pride filled me when she said that. I took a few wobbly steps closer to her, hungry now. Searching for the source of the sweet smell of her milk and finding it, I filled my belly while she crooned to me.

"Son, look at the big star over there. That is the North Star, and should you ever lose your way, it will guide you home. It is a constant in the night sky and is there even on the nights when the moon disappears."

"It's beautiful, Mother. What is north?" I asked.

"Only a direction, son. If you know where north is, then you will not get lost. See the sky lightening over there? That is east, and it is where the sun always comes up. Opposite east is west, and that is the direction where the sun goes down."

"What is that direction?" I said, pointing my nose to the opposite of north.

"That is south, son. The birds go south in the winter and come north in the spring. It is early spring. That is why you hear the birds now," Mother said. "If you know how to read the stars, moon, sun and wind, you will always know how to find your way."

The birds were singing. The frost was gone from the ground. The large round, golden sun was over the horizon now. The sweet grass smelled wonderful, and I was hungry again. Mother was nuzzling and teaching me about bugs. "Ticks can cause all sorts of diseases, and horse flies bite, causing big bumps like bees. Black flies are a real nuisance too. You must remember that grass, clover, and alfalfa are suitable for horses to eat, little one. Stay away from ryegrass, Johnson grass, and clover when it is moldy. These things will make you sick. Don't eat elderberry, milkweed, or foxglove, for they are deadly to horses."

I was listening to her because she told me that it was necessary for me to remember. "Mom, I'm hungry. Why can't I eat now and learn later?"

"You can eat again in a moment, son. First you need to learn."

A sound was coming from the north. Her whole body was frozen and rigid now, but as the noisy red thing passed us, she relaxed.

"Mom, what was that?" I asked.

"The men call that a truck. Most times they don't bother me. Today I suspect them."

"Why?" I asked.

"One day soon, one of them will come for us. Don't be frightened. We may not have much time together. So shush and listen to me. These things are all necessary for you to learn."

Increasingly nervous as the day wore on, she was now reeking of anxiety and worry. Still she stuffed my mind with too many things. "Look at the herd over there in that field. Watch how they play together. Do you see how the alpha mare finds the best food for her herd? Can you see the alpha male standing watch as the others graze and play? It's his job to protect the herd from predators—the same as it's the alpha mare's responsibility to find the best food."

Excited to see others of my kind, I nickered, though not fully understanding what she was telling me.

"Listen carefully. It might be your responsibility to protect the herd from coyotes and wolves when you grow up. Men can also be terrible predators, though I have heard that some of them are extremely loyal friends to horses. I don't have personal experience with that, son. Don't judge all men by what you may see and learn in the beginning."

"What are men, Mom, and why do I need to worry about them? Won't you be there to protect me?"

"I hope you are blessed, little one, and find a home and humans who love you and understand horses. I wish we could be together longer, but the men will come."

At last she let me eat. Her distress and torment lessened as the day turned to night.

"It seems we will have a little more time together, son. I don't want you to be alarmed when the men come and take you away from me. Please understand I am only a nurse mare and an old one at that. No matter how much I pray to the horse gods, nothing will stop the men from separating us."

"Why will they take me away, Mom? I don't want to leave you. Who will take care of me?" I asked.

"We will be divided soon. It might be a day or a week, but it will happen. And then I will be forced to nurse another foal. It has happened too many times before. I will try to fight to keep you, and as much as I want to say it will be different this time, I know better. Even the first time, when I was a young filly so many babies ago, fighting didn't help. The men are bigger, stronger, and have strange things that stop me. You must be brave and hold your head up, little one. Above all, don't listen to them if you hear them call you a junk foal; remember I said it was not true. I'm older now,

15

son, and someday will no longer be needed by these men. Once I can no longer breed and supply milk, they will free me. Then I'll watch over you the best I can."

"Where will you go, Mother? Will you come find me?" I asked.

"I will watch you from afar the best I can, son," she said softly. "Most importantly no matter what they say or do, keep it in your mind that you are a remarkably smart horse and better than most horses. Now sleep, little one. Tonight I'm here to take care of you."

Looking up at her, I saw her white coat gleaming in the night. The little gray around the top of her hooves seemed to melt into the darkness of the grass. Her words frightened me, but being young I didn't understand why they made me worry. Lying on the fresh grass feeling protected, I watched the movements of the clouds overhead and the bright lights of the stars. Finally I slept while she stood over me.

Later that night we roamed the field. Mother ate the grass and I nursed. Heavy clouds hid the moon and the stars from us. A light mist rose like a blue haze from the ground. A chill hung in the air, and a bitter-sweet feeling of regret mixed with love emanated from her. Even her milk tasted of it. She didn't talk any more that night, nor did she try to teach me. She just kept me close to her, nuzzling me.

It was a lovely morning when dawn broke. Streaks of red and gold covered the eastern sky. The song birds were rushing to and fro getting their meals. Squirrels and chipmunks were running up and down the trees.

Over the horizon, two small creatures were coming toward us. They looked so little, like ants, except that they walked on two legs and didn't crawl on the ground. They ambled toward us with a clumsy gait; there was no trace of gracefulness in their walk. The closer they came the more I could feel Mother's fear grow—she stank of it. I was so hungry, but she wouldn't allow me to eat. Instead she pushed me behind her trying to protect me the best she could.

"The men are here, son." she said. As they came closer, I saw the two-legged creatures were enormous. The closer they came, the smaller Mother became. Her fur was all puffed up and her ears were back. She smelled of terror and determination, which frightened me.

The men reeked of strange smells—meat, cigarettes, and coffee mixed with last night's beer—and walked awkwardly on their two legs. Still they came closer and closer. One of them was carrying something long and black.

"Please, let me keep this one. He is really exceptional, and I believe he will be my last baby," Mother said as she ran at them screaming.

Hearing one of the men yell, "Drug her," my whole world narrowed into darkness. The light of the new day, the smell of the grass, and the song of the birds disappeared. A loud horrific noise filled the early morning air, and I turned to flee. For a moment, it felt as if Mother was with me, but realizing she wasn't, I turned just in time to watch her legs wobble and see her fall slowly to the ground.

Trembling with fear, I started to make my way back to her. Was she dead? No, her chest still rose and fell. Something that looked like a bird feather stuck out of the side of her neck.

She was whimpering a desperate goodbye and gazing at me with love and grief, "I tried, son. Remember I will be with you always."

Something grabbed me and pulled so tightly I could hardly breathe. It was choking me and I fought to get away. One of the men held me tightly with a rope around my neck. He pulled me away from Mother. I could smell his sweat along with the stink of him. There was no tenderness or mercy in his hands. The other man was talking into the small black thing he held in one of his hands. Curtly he said, "Come in. We are ready."

Still I struggled to get away and watched as a monster came into view over the horizon. It made a loud growling noise. It didn't walk on two legs or four, nor did it fly like the birds or crawl on the ground like the worms and the bugs. It rolled on six wheels. It stank of smoke, fear, and death, and it was coming closer. I didn't know how to puff up and rear. I was too small to fight. I couldn't protect us. I just sobbed.

"Joe, grab his back end." One of the men said as they picked me up and tossed me into the back of the trailer. Before the door closed, scared and alone, I watched Mother get slowly to her feet, crestfallen, and head hanging low. As the men slammed the door and locked me into the box, I screamed, "Mama."

*T*hree

The Trip

Poor little foal lost and alone
Trapped in a trailer all forlorn
None to care if he lives or dies
Dinky fears the coming sunrise

Terrified for my life, I was flung to the floor and
against the walls so many times by the movement of this
box I was trapped in. I was afraid to try standing again,
so I cowered in the corner. On the floor of the trailer was
a bed of soiled straw. I lay there watching the sunlight
crawl across the dirty brown walls. The shadows from
the sun hitting the bars in the window looked like
enormous fingers coming to get me as they crept across
the walls of the trailer.

No longer was I able to see the grass, the sky, or
Mother. I lay there trembling and alone with no one to
love or cuddle me—just this large space all around me
that smelled of old manure, urine, fear, and death. Some
of the smell was my own fright. The stench was so

strong it made me sick. Where were they taking me? Without Mother to protect, nuzzle, and teach me, how would I survive? I felt so helpless.

My misery and my deep need to belong and feel loved were so strong, the solitude of my mind wandered back to the same questions. What would happen to me? Who would teach me? Would I get a chance to live as she promised? "Remember her words," I told myself.

"Hold your head up, son, you must be strong."

With every fiber of my being, I held on to her voice in my mind. It helped to ease the apprehension, the hunger, and the throbbing from my bruises.

The movement of this box stopped. When they opened the door, I was crouching in the back corner of the trailer like a weakling. One of the men held a bucket in his hand and the other the other a rope. The smell coming from the bucket made my stomach rumble. Even through my fright and the fury I smelled on these men, my stomach growled. There was no place to escape from even the dirtiest of these men.

Both of them were dirty, unshaven, and wearing blue jeans and sweat stained t-shirts. Joe's whole face was covered in hair. I could barely see his eyes through all the hair as he crouched down beside me. The other man once again put the rope around my neck and held my head in a forceful grip. Without so much as a kind word, the man called Joe stuck his fingers into the pail and forced them into my mouth. Not even the nasty taste of his grubby fingers stopped me from tasting the flavor of the milky stuff.

Hungrily I found myself sucking his dirty fingers. Several times the exercise was repeated. I sensed the resentment in these men even as they pushed my head down into the bucket. Famished, I drank greedily.

Impatiently the men pulled the bucket away from me and carried it out the door. Still hungry, I whimpered.

The man who put the rope around my neck complained as he slammed the door, "Stupid junk foal. I don't know why we always get stuck with this job, do you, Joe?"

The way he said junk foal made me cringe. It sounded as if he was talking about a piece of garbage. Holding my head up even in my dread, I let my mother's words again run through my mind. "Remember, do not pay any attention if you hear the words junk foal. These are words used by ignorant humans." For a little while, letting her voice play in my mind helped ease my panic.

It was fully dark, and not even a shadow could be seen in this huge container. The box stood still as they came in with the bucket. This time I didn't wait for the man's dirty fingers. Instead, when he set the pail on the floor, without hesitation I put my head in and drank. I nearly got my fill before they took it away again. I didn't try to beg them to let me go home. I knew they were deaf to my pleas. They didn't care.

Fighting off my loneliness, I tried to remember her teachings. "Think of the warmth of the sun, the beauty of the stars, the sound of thunder in the distance," I told myself.

Unfortunately, the roar of the truck made it difficult to think. "I suppose it doesn't matter. It doesn't make sense anyway. The sun and stars are only pictures in my mind," I whispered to the walls. I was barely able to hear myself over the drone of the motor.

My anguish was getting to me. The solitude and need for love and warmth was too deep. I wondered with the smell of death around me would I, like others before me, die in this rolling box? My young legs were wobbly from fear. I was still bumping into the walls and falling down, though it was much easier to stay on my hooves than it was when they first put me in this trailer. I knew that some of the stink in here was from my own panic and waste.

The future seemed bleak without Mother. Now that I didn't even have the sunlight keeping me company or the patterns on the walls, the loneliness was brutal. Even though I could see a little in the darkness of this box, each sound that was different from the drone of the engine echoed off the walls and made me jump. I was hungry.

We stopped again, and again the doors opened. The men's anger filled the box. There was a light shining in on me. I couldn't see because it blinded me, but I could smell the bucket, and my stomach growled in spite of my horror. Because I couldn't see the men, the sound of their boots coming toward me frightened me even more. I froze in my corner.

"Joe, hurry up and get in here. I don't want to waste any more time than necessary. Don't know why we have to do all this feeding anyway. It's just a stupid junk foal. It isn't like it's worth much."

"Harry, your animosity isn't helping me any. What does it matter to us anyway? They pay us by the hour. They must have their reasons for keeping these dumb foals in decent condition. Maybe it makes them worth more at the tanners. We're almost there now. Only a few more hours and we're home free. Then you can have all the beer you want."

"Just get over here, will you, and help me. Stop the jabbering; small as he is, he's scared. He might bite or put up a fight. It may still take two of us."

Finally they crouched down beside me. My stomach felt as if it was tearing a hole through me. The milky stuff smelled like heaven. I was unable to think of anything else, so I drank. With only their irritation around me, it felt like a rock falling into my gut. My instinct to live was strong, so I continued drinking. All too soon the bucket was ripped away from me. Still hungry, I tried to reach it, but the one called Joe held me securely. Soon I was shut back in the box with only the echo of their hatred and the darkness to keep me company again.

I cried, "Mama, where are you?" But I got no answer to my pleas; they just reverberated off the walls. The straw was even more soiled now from my own waste, and I was forced to lay in it. Would this hell never end?

Would I ever see the sun, feel the wind in my mane, or smell the grass again? Perhaps my life would be spent in this moving box longing for the sound of the birds, the scent of the field, and the beauty of the clouds moving across the sky. Oh, I missed those things. How lonesome it was without the sense of belonging. "I'm too young to be alone," I sobbed.

Four

The Barn

A pact is made between the two
Friends forever, never adieu

The truck finally stood still, and this time the drone of the motor stopped. The men opened the door. I couldn't see. Heavy cloud cover hid the moon and stars. After spending so many hours in the dark, the bright lights in the yard blinded me. The sound and smell of the crowd of noisy humans seemed to fill up the space. I crouched in the corner of the trailer.

The men didn't lift me this time—not like they did when they threw me into the box. Instead, they put that same dirty rope they used before around my neck. Downward they pulled me into what seemed like an overwhelmingly large crowd of humans.

A male human took my rope and led me into a small yard where the smells were better. The smell of death was gone; in its place was the clean smell of farm

27

life. In front of the barn stood a woman in a billowing red skirt, "Dinky little thing isn't he? He sure smells terrible," she said to the man.

"They always do when they get here don't they?" he answered.

I heard other animals calling, "Who are you?"

Still fearful and unsteady, I held my head up high and called back, "I am beautiful and strong. My mother told me so."

So loud were the humans, I could barely hear their replies, but I thought I heard them laughing at me. That made me sad.

The man leading me wore blue from head to toe. Deeper into the dark barn he led me. Finally he pushed me into a small room with little patience for my unsteady legs or for the bruises that covered my body from falling.

In the dim light of the room, I heard a voice, "Hi. My name is Lucky. What's your name?"

Afraid, tired, and hungry, I asked, "I don't know, Lucky. How do you get a name?"

"Oh, sooner or later they'll call you something. Then you'll know your name," he said.

"Then I guess my name is Dinky, because that's what they called me." I couldn't manage anything more. Before looking around the room, I went over and drank some of the water in the pail. "I'm hungry."

"There will be nothing more till morning," Lucky said, licking my wounds and comforting me while I cried. We snuggled close and slept. Each time I woke up weeping, he calmed me down and reassured me.

Cock-a-doodle-doo filled the room. It was the strangest sound I ever heard. "What's that noise, Lucky?"

"It's called Mac Rooster, and he's greeting the dawn and telling everyone it's time to get up. We'll get our breakfast soon now. It always comes after Mac Rooster calls," Lucky said.

Lucky wasn't my mother, nor was he an adult horse. He was too young to teach me manners or the ways of the herd, yet he'd been here longer and knew things I could learn. He was bigger than me and brown. With him near, I felt a measure of safety. Each day at the farm shortly after Mac Rooster called, they brought us our breakfast. For a while they only brought us the milky stuff, but soon the humans began putting hay and grain in our room along with our pail of milk.

"Dinky, I overheard the humans talking. Soon they won't give us the bucket. If you don't learn to eat hay and grain, you'll die."

So each day I tried to chew it, but it didn't seem natural. "Lucky, are you sure it's normal for us to eat this when we're so young?"

He just grunted and went on eating. Sure enough, the next morning the humans put only water in our bucket. Gone was the milky stuff.

Our room was old and smelled of other horses even through the thin layer of new shavings on the floor. That morning we woke to rain. It came down exceptionally hard, so instead of taking us out into the little yard, they tied us up inside the.

"Lucky, this is horrible just standing here unable to move around. Even being in the little room is better. I like it best when they put us out into the little yard, don't you?"

"Yes, Dinky, but I heard the woman say if we get sick we will be worth nothing, and they will have wasted their time and money on us. So we have to stay in here if it's raining," Lucky answered.

"I guess we are fortunate not to be on the cross ties. See those chains hanging over there on the wall, Dinky?

Ole Jack told me, they are called cross ties and humans hook the chains one on each side of a horses halter. Then the horse must stand still, held between them, unable to move around much at all. We are too little for halters, so they tie us up instead."

"I don't think I would like cross ties Lucky. It is bad enough having a rope around my neck and tied to the post. Why do you suppose the rope is tied so high? I feel like my neck is being stretched off my head."

"Me too Dinky, I don't know why the rope is up so high though. I think it would be worse though to be on the cross ties."

"What are halters Lucky?"

"I don't know, Dinky, all I understood was they are something that covers the face. It doesn't sound nice at all."

Each day I learned a little more about life on the farm. "Dinky, don't try to socialize with the chickens. They're snobs and only like to talk amongst themselves. Besides Ole Jack told me they were just big gossips anyway."

I wondered if there was something more to it, but I didn't think Lucky would know. Maybe if I was here long enough, the chickens would talk to me, I thought as the woman led us out to the little yard.

"Hi, young'uns. How's it going?" a strange looking little light-brown fellow with horns on his head and whiskers on his chin yelled from across the fence.

"There's Ole Jack now," Lucky said. "We better go over and talk to him, or else there'll be too much ruckus, and they might not let us stay out in the sun today, Dinky.

"Howdy, Ole Jack. Where have you been?" Lucky asked as he trotted over to the fence.

"They lent me to another farm for breeding. Woo hoot, did I have a grand time, little ones. Who's your buddy, Lucky?" Ole Jack asked.

"This is my new friend, Dinky."

"Is he okay? Looks a little skinny and wobbly to me, Lucky."

"Yah, Ole Jack, Dinky is still recovering from the trip and losing his mother."

"Ah, another nurse mare's foal, eh, Lucky? Hi, Dinky, welcome to the farm. I advise you not to get too comfortable here."

"Why's that, Ole Jack? And what's breeding?" I asked shyly.

"Well, your mothers were bred to a stallion, and you were born. Your mothers were nurse mares. Unfortunately, a nurse mare is only useful for the milk she produces, which is why you were taken away from her. Her milk was needed to feed another horse's foal. You two are just a byproduct of the breeding.

"Nurse mare foals have no real purpose. You're not much use here on the farm. Chickens give eggs, goats and cows give milk, but the humans here think they can make a little money by selling you. Likely you'll both end up at the meat market or the tanners. There are a whole group of humans here today. Likely as not, one of them will buy you, if not now then next time."

"Does that mean I'll never see my mother again?" I asked.

"I expect you won't, Dinky," Ole Jack said.

I started to cry. At least I understood why we were separated, though it didn't make the separation any easier.

"Now don't cry, youngster," Ole Jack tried to console me. "It's just the way of the world."

I tried to think of something else instead. "What's a tanner, Ole Jack?" I asked, because he seemed to know a lot.

"I don't want to frighten you two, but a tanner is where they take the hide off your back and make bags and shoes for humans to wear."

"But what does that mean? How could they take my hide without me dying? I don't think it's possible to live without it. What are bags and shoes anyway?" I asked.

"Dinky, calm down. I said I don't want to frighten you, but it's true. You'd die if they took your hide. Bags are what humans carry things around in, and shoes go on their feet." Ole Jack answered.

"I don't want to die! I don't want to have my hide taken to make bags or shoes, and I certainly don't want to be eaten," I said tartly.

"You sure are a sassy little fellow aren't you? Maybe that will help you survive. Sometimes, you nurse mare foals find homes. You might become one of the privileged ones, but I recommend you don't count on it. I don't want you to get your hopes up, little ones. You won't stay here long."

Changing the subject, Lucky piped in, "How's everything with you, Ole Jack?"

"Same old, same old, Lucky. You know, the other animals are already taking bets on which of you little ones will be the first to ship out. Oh, don't you go putting your ears back and giving me sass, Dinky. Life is what it is, and we all need our amusements."

"Ole Jack doesn't mean us any harm. We got to go, Ole Jack. Glad to hear you had a good time at the breeding. Dinky and I want to stretch our legs. See you later."

"Bye, young'uns. Dinky, don't take what I say too hard. I'm a grumpy old goat, and I tell it the way it is. You two younglings go enjoy your bit of sun before the humans come to get you. See you later. Ta ta."

It was hard after that to enjoy the sun, and thinking about it made it impossible for me to sleep. Lucky, ever the optimist, wouldn't discuss Ole Jack's words that day. He just soaked in the sun and enjoyed the moment.

The little yard had an old brown fence that kept us separated from the other farm animals. There was a small patch of sun, a bit of warm dirt to lie on, and a bucket of water hanging on the fence.

I came out of my reverie when I heard the sound of the humans coming. I wished they would leave us out longer. The sun felt so lovely on my back, but it wasn't to be today.

The humans soon came and dragged us over to the hard dirt round about. I realized I'd gotten my wish to stay out in the sun longer. I truly needed to learn to be more specific, I thought. Lucky and I looked in horror at the sight before us. The round dirt circle was packed full of strange humans, just as Ole Jack had said.

"What's going on, Lucky?" I whispered.

"Shush, this is an inspection, Dinky. Don't be afraid," he said quivering.

The dirt beneath our feet was hard and hot as they tied us to the railing along the side of the road. Lucky was first. I watched as they pulled him into the middle of the circle. It looked like there were hundreds of people taking turns poking him, putting their fingers in his mouth, and picking up his feet. How horrible, I thought as I stood there unable to get away. Even though it was sunny, it seemed the entire world had narrowed to this little patch of dirt.

Finally the woman brought Lucky back and tied him up to the rail. I shivered watching her walk toward me. I didn't think I could handle what I just saw happening to Lucky. It was worse than I imagined it would be when I watched them mess with Lucky. A really dirty, stinky man forced his filthy fingers into my mouth; they tasted nasty—worse even than Joe's fingers had been. After all, he had just been playing with

Lucky's feet. He felt all around inside my mouth. I
couldn't bite him; he was pulling my tongue and playing
with my teeth. Then someone else picked up my feet.
Finally, they were done with me and I was led back to
Lucky.

Once again we stood tied at the rail watching the
humans speculate about us. I heard two of them making
a wager about which market Lucky and I would go to.
One of the women loudly proclaimed that my hide
would make a beautiful bag.

Shivering and shaking, the man and woman led us
back to our room. We could still hear the crowd of
humans in the yard. They seemed to be laughing and
joking. "Does anyone want a cup of coffee or a beer?" I
heard the man yell as he left the barn.

Feeling degraded, Lucky and I remained silent. We
listened to the noise out in the yard and looked at each
other. Eventually I asked, "Lucky, have you ever been
through that before?"

"Once, before you came, Dinky. There weren't so
many people that time."

"Lucky," I cried, "Did you hear what that woman
said? I don't want to be a bag, even if it's a beautiful

one. Why are they so mean? Mother told me I'd have a home and a family. Do you think we'll find homes?"

He didn't answer me. He never did when I asked these questions. He only grunted and nuzzled closer.

Five

The Women

Our motto will be
Together at least
Through thick and through thin
No matter how bad
We'll make it alright

Except for the hour or so a day in the little yard, we had no place to stretch our muscles. Instead we spent most of our time locked in this dark little room. The windows were too high and we couldn't see out, so we took turns lying in the little bit of sun that bounced off the dirty old walls of our cell. It wasn't that we were treated horribly at the farm. Mostly the humans paid little attention to us except on parade day. They didn't pet us or talk to us. They just pushed or pulled us around when necessary. I don't think they knew we had feelings. If they did, it didn't matter to them anyway.

"Lucky, how long were you with your mother? Did she teach you about the ticks that bite and cause all sorts of diseases and how a bee's bite really stings?"

"No, Dinky, my mother didn't teach me anything. I think she must have been younger than yours. After all, we had a bit more time together than you did with your mom. Surely she would have taught me if she had been an older mare and more used to losing her young. At least, I hope that's why she didn't teach me," Lucky answered sadly.

That morning we saw other horses in the distance. Unless the wind was blowing just right, they were too far away for us to hear them. As we watched, the men took another foal away, and we remembered our mothers.

Trying to brighten the mood, I told Lucky what my mother had told me about how a herd works. "My mother told me that the alpha mare finds the best food for the herd, and the alpha male protects the herd from predators," I said, trying to explain the ways of the herd.

"Oh, Dinky, shut up. I think you're making all this up, and I'm tired of hearing about it. You were too little when you left your dam to remember these things, so don't go on and on. Maybe if we watch, we'll learn the truth."

So I shut up. Lucky seldom got angry with me, but when he did it hurt.

The humans had a dog named Smitty. Before I ever saw him, I learned it was vital to stay away from him.

"I'm not sure why, but he doesn't like horses or goats. He always tries to challenge us. He runs up behind us to bite our legs. I guess we just have to be faster. Dinky, Ole Jack told me that Smitty once bit a foal so badly he had to be put down."

"What does put down mean, Lucky?"

Lucky squirmed a bit before answering. "They kill you right then and there, Dinky."

Before I could respond, Lucky went on. "Ole Jack expects Smitty is jealous. I haven't seen him yet, but I've smelled him. He smells unclean and of meat. I'm glad the humans don't let him run loose on this side of the farm much."

"If we're out in the little yard and he comes around, how will we get away from him, Lucky? There's nowhere to hide."

"I guess we'll need to try to protect each other, Dinky, and hope that will work."

That morning, a red truck pulled into the yard, and two women in blue jeans climbed out of it. I was a bit over two months old, and Lucky was three months. It would be my second trip to the parade grounds. We stood tied at the rail as the two women looked us over. There was something remarkably different about these women. Instead of poking and prodding us, they talked sweetly to us and tried to pet us. It was very strange.

These were the first kind words either of us had ever heard a human speak. Their hands were gentle, and they smelled of horses, grass, and flowers. After looking us over, we were taken back to our stall, and the two women went inside the house. They hadn't checked our teeth or played with our feet.

"I'm confused, Lucky. Is there something different about these women?"

He just looked at me. We heard them leave the house after a while. They stopped at our little stall to let us sniff them again before they drove away. Even though I knew they were different, I pinned my ears back. I was still afraid of them.

"Dinky, I think you're right. There's something special about these women," Lucky stated.

It didn't matter. They left and we were alone again wondering about our fate. They weren't like the other people who had come to view us. They didn't speak about meat markets, auctions, shoes, and bags. They talked about how cute we were and whether they could help us grow and find us decent homes. They didn't stay long though, and all too soon the women became a hazy a memory.

We hadn't had the milk in our buckets for quite some time and were eating grain and hay on a regular basis when the two women came back. "Cathy, you hold them while I put them in their halters," Alice said. They put these things over our heads, around our noses, and under chins. At first it frightened us to have our faces partly covered, and both Lucky and I fought a little. However, the women were bigger than we were, and soon we each sported a halter.

The women led us up a ramp into another trailer that was hooked onto the back of their truck. Remembering the trailer that brought me to this farm, I fought them a bit before they got me into it. This one was cleaner and there was fresh hay on the floor.

"Where are we going? Are we going to the meat market, the auction, or to the place where they take our hides to make bags and shoes like Ole Jack said?" I whimpered.

Lucky didn't reply. He just kept on eating the hay on the floor.

"I'm so thin, Lucky. They won't find much meat on me, so it will probably be the place where they make the bags and shoes. Remember what that one woman said, 'His hide will make a beautiful bag.'"

"Dinky, don't be afraid. These women tried to pet us and said we were cute. Remember they talked about finding us homes." Lucky's words didn't help.

As the doors shut, I heard Ole Jack yell, "Good luck, little ones. Maybe you'll be fortunate. I'll hope for you."

I found it hard to be optimistic. Too many unpleasant things had already happened to me. I wasn't prepared to believe in the possibility of good things. Could we trust these women and believe they would give us a home? I was still unsure of them even though they seemed kind. Perhaps, finding a home was only another story, like my mother rescuing me. I was afraid I wouldn't have a chance to grow strong and beautiful and learn the ways of the herd. It didn't matter what Lucky tried to tell me. I was skinny and weak with anxiety and lack of food. I was small for my age, and my fur was quite matted from lack of grooming. We had tried to rub our winter coats off against the walls of our stall, but it wasn't the same as having solid ground underfoot to roll in. The walls didn't take the dead fur off of us the way a decent roll would.

We didn't know much about humans. Our only experience with them was shoving a bucket under our nose, putting a rope around our necks, or dragging us out and parading us in front of other smelly humans who said cruel things. Our experience only told us they'd shut us in a small stall away from sunlight and clean air.

"Lucky, my mother told me that she heard some humans are friends to horses. How will we know if these women will comfort us?" Were there actually humans who were devoted to horses? Could any of them understand horse as we understood some of their language? Please, I didn't want to lose Lucky, my only friend, as I lost my mother. I didn't want to have to be alone and bereft again. The trailer was slowing down, and we were stopping again.

The door opened, and they came in to check on us. They made sure we had water and hay and checked to make sure we weren't hurt. "Aren't they cute?" Alice said as she tried to pet us.

Anxious, I bared my teeth and put my ears back. I knew they were different, but I didn't know where we were going or if I could trust them or any human. I watched them walk out of the trailer.

"You must eat, Dinky," Lucky tried to coax me.

It was no use. I was too worried.

Six

The Stable

A room of their own
Fresh air and sunlight
These little lost foals
Could run with the light

"Something's happening, Lucky. Can you feel the trailer slowing down?" Both of us had trouble standing. We were flung against each other, even though the trailer was now moving at a snail's pace. Gone was the smooth ride we'd experienced since leaving the farm that morning. In its place was a jarring movement. The trailer bumped over the ruts in the road.

The sun was lower in the sky, but still held enough light for us to see. While they led us off the trailer, we looked around. In the distance there were green fields. In each field was a horse with its own shelter. The smell of horses and dogs was strong in the air. At the bottom of the ramp were many humans. Their voices sounded full of excitement.

Across the road was a small field with a little shelter. In front of us loomed a large red barn. Walking into the barn, we heard many horses calling, "Who are you?"

The crowd of humans standing around to view us seemed so large that Lucky and I were trembling with fear. Their voices were sweet and low, "Aren't the babies cute?"

"Look at the poor things."

Weary, famished, and frightened of what would come next, wanting only to eat and sleep, I put my ears back when one of them came too close.

Our new stall smelled sweet. On the floor was fresh hay. On the wall by the door hung a bucket of grain and next to it one of water. The humans talked to each other. Why couldn't they be quiet? I thought.

"Poor little ones. Look how skinny the black one is. I think we should name him Coal."

I wanted to yell at them, "My name is Dinky."

"They won't understand you," Lucky said. "Humans seem pretty stupid, Dinky. We can learn their language, but I have yet to meet one that understands horse."

Shut into the stall, we found it hard with all the human strangers staring at us through the bars to eat and settle down. Bright lights began flashing (from what we were later to learn was called a camera). The humans were so noisy; I couldn't tell what the horses in the other stalls were saying. I could barely even hear Lucky, who was braver than I was. He allowed the humans to pet and stroke him and put his cute face on.

"When will they leave us alone, Lucky? It seems like they've been staring at us for hours."

"It hasn't been that long. Soon we'll be able to eat and rest."

Finally the humans left, and we explored our new surroundings. Lucky and I took turns rolling in the fresh shavings. "I think we've been adopted, Dinky," Lucky said to me.

"What's adopted?" I asked.

He just grunted at me and went on eating. When supper was over we told each other stories. It was our favorite past time, and one that held us together at the farm in that dark room. We made up stories of all the incredible things that might happen in the coming days.

"Lucky, maybe we'll even have a field to play in, like the one we saw across the road, and a place where we can run and lay in the sun. Did you see it, the one with the little shelter with the blue thing on top? I bet it would be an excellent place to stay when it rained. Maybe it's what my mother meant when she was telling me how to find shelter."

"Dinky, go to sleep. I expect tomorrow we'll find out if we get a field. It would be lovely though if we could spend the day outside and not stuck in a room."

Both of us were so drowsy we could barely stand, so we snuggled up against each other and slept. We both dreamed we had fields to run and play in, mothers to teach us the ways of the herd, strong stallions to protect us, and plenty of food and safety.

Dreaming again of my mother, I told her about Lucky and the place we were in now. I told her of the nice women that took us from the farm and that I hoped we'd found a home.

She nuzzled, loved, and told me, "Remember my words, Dinky. The hard times may not be over yet, and if you are to survive you must eat, grow strong, and remember the things I taught you."

The sun was up. I woke with my mind filled with the sound of her words.

Lucky looked at me long and hard after I told him about my dream and said, "Dinky, don't worry so much. We have a home now."

I wasn't sure I trusted his opinion, but I believed I should remember my mother's words. I was sure that somehow my mother visited me in my dreams and she was still watching over me. Somehow she had sent me a true prophecy of things to come.

The stable was up early. We heard the movement and calling of one horse to another and smelled the grain and the hay as each horse was fed. Soon our turn came, and they brought us a bucket of grain and some hay to share. Because he was bigger, Lucky ate more than I did. The women talked to us softly and sweetly while they fed us and let us get their scent.

When breakfast was over, they led us out into the same little field I'd seen from the road the night before. It was the one with the big blue tarp instead of a roof on top to keep the rain out of the shelter. There was green stuff growing in the field, but extremely little grass. It was soft to walk, run, and lay on, but not acceptable to eat. Three buckets of water hung on the fence. Somehow with six of us in the little field, it didn't seem enough.

Star, one of the other foals in the field, saw us looking at the buckets and said, "Unfortunately, by mid-day they'll all be quite empty, and we'll be a bit thirsty till the end of the day when we go back to our stalls. They won't be filled again until tomorrow."

The little field was large enough for us to sunbathe, run, and play. We didn't have to stay in the stall all day and night anymore. I loved to feel the sun on me and the breeze in my mane, watch the birds fly overhead, and feel the rain on my back—as long it wasn't raining too heavily. The sounds of the traffic on the road frightened us at first, but Star said, "Soon you'll become accustomed to it."

It was just as she said. Soon Lucky and I began to enjoy watching the comings and goings from the barn.

We spent the morning learning each other's scent and sharing secrets. We took turns telling each other the story of how we lost our mothers. All of us had suffered a similar fate. This didn't seem like a coincidence to me. How strange it would be if all of us sharing this little field had the same experiences. I didn't believe it to be accidental.

One night just before we went to our stalls for supper, some humans took Star away. The field felt emptier without her. She was the third foal to leave it. Now it was only Lucky, Kaylee, and me in the field.

Kaylee was already adopted, but was living at the barn. She was a pretty little filly. Her coat looked as if it was painted gold, brown, and white. The three of us were fast friends clinging to each other now with all the other foals gone. Except, of course, when Kaylee was with her humans; then it was just Lucky and me. We were nearly inseparable and did everything together.

Kaylee's humans came to take her for a walk again. She would eat sweet grass and get extra meals and treats. Her family would brush and pet her till her coat was shiny. Lucky and I were a bit jealous of her; she looked so healthy and pretty.

"Lucky, soon Kaylee will be back. I hate it when she brags. See, here she comes now." Sure enough, soon we were listening to her boast again.

"My human said they were going to buy me a saddle with pretty bells when I get bigger."

"What's a saddle, Kaylee?" I asked.

She didn't answer and just continued on, "I got to eat the sweet grass, and they gave me some little candy treats. Then they brushed me, and it felt really good."

It was always the same with her, "I got to do this, and I got to do that. My humans said this and my humans said that." It was really quite a nuisance to listen to.

We just turned and walked away. As usual, Lucky and I didn't socialize with Kaylee for the rest of that day, even though she looked quite dejected.

Perhaps Lucky was right and humans were pretty stupid. They didn't appear to understand horses or realize horses didn't like the green stuff in the little field. It tasted bitter and made our stomachs sour if we ate it. I suspected they thought the green stuff was enough for us to eat during the day. Although we spent most of the day hungry, we were happy.

Humans seemed to talk nonstop. They talked about a lot of strange things. Many of them had nothing to do with horses, though we listened closely. I heard Alice's little girl ask, "Cathy, do you think there are horses in heaven?"

Curious about heaven, I asked, "Lucky, do you think this is heaven? We have all this sunshine and room to run and play. We can even take sunbaths in this field if we want."

Lucky and Kaylee looked at me. "No, Dinky," Kaylee butted in. "It's close, but it can be much better. I get to go for walks with my humans, eat sweet grass, and get treats. They brush, pet, and kiss me. That's heaven, Dinky. This is only a tiny slice of it."

I looked at her with disgust. I was tired of her bragging. It was nice to hear what it felt like to have a human family, but I could do without her smugness. I turned, walked away, and lay down in the sun to bathe. I overheard Kaylee ask Lucky what she did wrong this time, but I fell asleep before hearing his answer.

On another day, strange humans came to visit. Lucky was much braver than me. He stood quietly, put on a cute face, and allowed them to pet and stroke him. Of the three of us, I was the smallest. Nevertheless, I was still determined to grow larger. Even though the humans called me Coal, in my heart I'd always be Dinky.

After supper, they led us into a big room inside the barn. I was shaking because I was so scared. Was this to be another inspection where people would poke and prod us and talk about auctions, shoes, and bags? As Cathy led me alongside Alice and Lucky, they continued to chat, as was normal for humans.

"Alice," Cathy said. "Carmen said it's time for them to learn socialization."

"I know she is right, we need them to learn to trust people and learn the ways of the stable." Alice replied.

"She told me that we need to get them adoptable." Cathy responded. "Carmen said they can't stay here forever."

Not liking the sound of that, I went and hid behind Cathy. She was one of the women who took us from the farm and brought us here. I was losing trust for these women who smelled of horses and talked to us sweetly. Once again I was afraid and nervous. Maybe one day they'd turn on us too. How could we be sure?

Alice and Cathy continued to lead Lucky and me around the big room. As we walked, they talked, and I looked around. The big room was crowded with humans walking horses.

Back in our room, I asked Lucky, "What do you suppose that was all about?"

"Dinky, please learn to enjoy the moment. Listen to what they have to teach us, so we can get our own humans like Kaylee and not go to the meat market or the auction. You must grow strong, Dinky," he declared even as he pushed me from the bucket so he could have the larger share of our food.

In spite of the fact that I was small for my age, timid, and always hungry, I hoped I was beginning to grow and fatten up a bit. But I wasn't growing as much as Lucky.

The rain came down extremely hard. The three of us stood under the shelter. There'd be no naps in the sun, nor would we get to play or exercise that day. I guess it would be a day to tell each other stories about the things we saw around us. Even with the heavy rain, it was better for us to be outside than stuck inside the small, dark room. At least we had things to look at, could smell the grass, and have the breeze in our manes.

"Lucky, there must be a better way for us to learn not to be frightened of humans touching and handling us," I said as I stood wrapped up in some shiny crinkly material I heard someone call cellophane. "I genuinely hate cellophane, but I'm no longer afraid to participate in these games. The bad woman said it's a part of the sacking out process. I don't know what that means, but I don't like the sound of it."

"Dinky, I don't like Carmen; I think she's a wicked woman. I know Cathy and all the other women listen to her when she gives us the lessons, but she frightens me."

"She scares me too, Lucky. I don't think she knows what is good for horses."

As we all stood there in our cellophane, Carmen said over the speaker, "If we want them all to be able to be adopted into decent homes, they must learn not to be frightened. Humans must be able to handle any part of the foal."

I tried to talk to Lucky about what Carmen said, but he just said, "Dinky, don't worry. We have a home, plenty of food, and people to love and take care of us now."

This sounded like another story, and I didn't believe Lucky was right. While he was growing bigger, I seemed to get thinner and hungrier all the time. It didn't seem like plenty of food to me. Maybe it was like my mother told me in those first hours, "You are extremely smart, Dinky." I heard the women. They always talked about the day we would be adopted and which of us would find a home first. This wasn't our forever home. Lucky was wrong. It didn't matter that we liked these women. They wouldn't let us stay here.

One day I overheard the women talking about the fair. Alice said, "Cathy, the fair has been going on since 1874. It draws people from all over the county. We can show them off there and find them homes."

As she walked past them, Carmen said, "Alice, they must find homes or go to auction. You know we have the other horses coming soon. Cute as they are, we don't have room for these little ones, they will have to go soon. I have a business to run here. Joan, did you worm the boarder's horses today?" Carmen yelled.

"Will we be worming the nurse mare foals soon Carmen?" The new woman Dolores asked."

"I believe they are still too young, Dolores." Carmen replied a bit crossly as she walked off.

Now I was sure, Lucky was wrong. This wasn't to be our forever home.

At lessons one night, Carmen said, "Alice, I think they're all ready to be weaned." That word had a horrible, ominous sound to it. It didn't matter what it meant. It was not a nice word. I knew it would mean more change and loss for me somehow.

There was an overall mood of anticipation among the women. A feeling of impending doom crept over me. It felt as if more changes were coming. I'd already suffered way too much. I'd had too much taken away from me to trust that their enthusiasm would lead to something good. Humans' excitement always seemed to mean terrible things to us horses.

Seven

The Fair

In sweltering heat
That day I did meet
The two who would be
A family to me

The heat came in waves one morning like nothing I had ever experienced before. Dolores came in and put our halters on us. Her excitement made me nervous. Then as she led us out of the barn, I saw it right in front of us. Waiting like an ogre, its doors open as if to swallow us, stood one of those nasty trailers. Although I could see there was hay on the floor for us to eat, it still stunk of fear, gasoline, and oil.

"This is a terrible sign, Lucky." I said. "It's an extremely distressing sign. Where are we going? Why do they have to make us leave our home? I don't feel ready for more changes, do you?" He was used to my constant worry and questions, so I got no answer. "Please, don't make us leave, we're just beginning to feel a little safe," I begged as I planted my hooves in front of the ramp. It was no use. They were bigger than me, and up the ramp I went.

Inside the trailer, it was even hotter. All told there were five of us—three horses, Lucky, and me—crammed into this sweat box. We were all nervous. All of us were brought to the stable by these same women a couple of months earlier. Each of us had begun to feel a measure of security in our surroundings after the trauma of losing our families. Unsure and troubled again, we waited for the fabric of our lives to be ripped apart once more.

The women had treated us kindly and genuinely seemed to care for us. They didn't know my belly was always hungry. Nor did they understand that we had a crawly feeling inside of us. It was probably some of those bad bugs my mother warned me about.

They were kind women. They didn't know that the corrupt woman who owned the stable couldn't be bothered with us. When she came around to look us over, we could tell she was ruthless. To her it didn't matter if we survived and grew up strong. I didn't think the nice women knew she was evil or that we had these crawly things inside of us. They tried their best to treat us kindly with love and to teach us how to be adoptable. They just didn't know enough about horses, and they listened to the bad woman instead of trying to learn to speak horse.

Fortunately, the trip was short. Outside the trailer, it was extremely loud. There were the sounds of other horses, farm animals, music, and all sorts of other strange noises. Some of them were so deafening they made us all jumpy. The smell of grass, machinery, and humans permeated the air. We could hardly hear the sound of our own breathing over the calls of one human to another, the banging of hammers, and metal against metal. Standing and waiting in the sweltering heat of the trailer, we could barely breathe in the stifling air.

"The women are putting up portable fencing and a tent," one of the bigger horses who could see through the window told us. "The tent is probably so they can be out of the sun during the day."

At last we were led off the trailer one by one. Sweat dripping from us, Lucky and I were the last to leave the trailer. They led the two of us into an extremely small enclosure standing next to the tent.

At first we enjoyed looking around at all the different things going on. The thrill soon passed, as there was no escape from the sun. Humans continued to stream by viewing, poking, and prodding us in the enclosure. Some of the little children were horrid. "Cute horsey," or "Cute pony, Mama," they said as they poked us again and again while their parents laughed. It was the hottest day I could ever remember. From just after dawn till sunset, we stood in that pen. I began to wonder if we were to spend our lives in this small space without room for either of us to lie down, move around, or get out of the sun.

Where would Lucky and I go if it rained? Still, we wished for rain to cool us down. We felt trapped and wondered how we could have a nap. The space was too little and the noise and constant parade of strange humans too great.

"Lucky, what's happened to the nice women? Why did they do this to us? Do you think we'll be adopted?"

He didn't answer me. He was afraid. Both of us were miserable. We didn't know what would happen. Maybe, if we were truly blessed, we would meet our forever families here at the fair. Was it possible? We wondered.

Eight

Misery

All alone in a cage
Paced the two little ones
Afraid of the auctions

It seemed like the days never ended, standing in that cage in the hot sun. The only breaks were at night when they loaded us into the trailer, and we went back to our stall to eat and sleep. The days seemed like years to us— the misery was so keen. Please, let it be over soon, I prayed. Let us have our little field and not ever have to go to the fair again.

We hated the fair. It was noisy and hot. Most of all, we detested the humans who came by. Each day the sun felt hotter, and our hooves were getting sore from the hard, searing ground. Would we ever again have nap time? The noise of the crowds, rides, and machinery had no appeal to us anymore. The smells of the oil and the sweat of humans became intolerable. Even the smell of

the sweet grass in the air was awful, because we
couldn't reach it. It was agony for us to stand there.

"Lucky, do you think this is auction?"

With despair in his eyes he looked at me and didn't
answer.

"Lucky, please, do you think we'll end up as meat
or shoes?"

Still nothing. He just got more panicky. Was he
afraid to answer for fear he would make one of these
horrible things become reality?

The good women spoke kindly to us once in a
while. Mostly they were too busy talking to the crowds
of humans that continued to come by and giggle at us.
We were mortified. Most of the time Lucky tried to put
on his cute face, but even he was tired of trying to be
nice to these awful people. Why were we here? What
was to happen to us? Would we ever go home again?
Where was home? If it was our little stall and field, then
why did these women bring us here to be poked,
prodded, and laughed at by every small two-legged
creature that came near? Why didn't they stop them if
they were sympathetic women? I didn't understand and
Lucky wouldn't speak to me. Maybe he was too upset to
communicate.

In the afternoon, the sun became so hot that fewer
and fewer humans came by. At least we were left alone.
Even the women stayed under their tent and talked to
each other. When humans did stop by, they talked to
them about us. I heard them say I was cute, but too small
and skinny to be a considered an acceptable horse. Many
of them asked if I was sick. Several of them were
interested in Lucky and said they might adopt him. None
of them seemed particularly interested in adopting me.
Only the small, horrid, little ones, who'd poke me and
say "cute horsey," or "pony, Mama," seemed to like me.
Please, don't let me end up with a human family who
will treat me this way, I prayed.

There were still a couple of people looking at the
bigger horses—the ones that had their own little fields
with grassy areas. Although they were in the hot sun too,
at least they had sweet grass in their little fields. The big
horses had room to get away from the people who came
by. Unlike Lucky and me, they could move around,
stretch their legs, or lie down if they wanted to nap. The
little bit of hay left from our meal was soiled, and our
water bucket empty. Still the women sat in the tent and
paid no attention to us. Did they even notice that our
bucket was empty?

Their voices droned on. Lucky and I were alone, hot, tired, crabby, and worried. Lucky was so petrified he wouldn't nuzzle or comfort me. He wouldn't talk to me. If I came too close or tried to talk to him, he put his ears back. It felt as if I'd lost everyone again. I was more alone than I'd been since being taken away from my mother and dragged into that first ghastly trailer. That loss was bad enough, but a second loss was harder. Was it always to be this way? Would I even survive the day? I wondered. If at least he would talk to me, it might be a bit easier. Even at night when we went back to our little stall, he wouldn't talk. He just ate and slept.

I'd miss him, but I hoped he'd get adopted. If he had a loving family, I would be happy for him. Now that my coat was dull and untidy, I probably wouldn't become a bag or shoes. Probably I'd end up as someone's supper, although it was hard to guess how they would find enough meat on me to eat.

It was our third day in that small caged place with the sun beating down on us. When would it end? Each day, we heard the women talk to the different humans about adopting us. It seemed they were all interested in Lucky. He looked so much bigger and stronger than me. So many humans asked if I was sick that I was beginning to worry. I knew I was skinny, little, hungry, and my belly felt like it had crawly things in it all the time. But was I sick?

Each night in our little stall after another horrid day, Lucky said, "Dinky, you worry too much." He'd go back to eating and then sleep. Other than those few words, Lucky didn't seem to want my company at all. He was my friend, and we loved each other. He was bigger and more likely to get adopted than I was. It seemed there was never enough food for both of us, and he looked so much better than I did. I thought he had less to worry about than me. After all, so many people asked about him at the fair. At night in our stall, the time flew by. We were scared the next day would come and we'd have to do it all again—get back into the trailer and go spend another day cooped up in that cage.

It was so miserable there standing in the hot sun with the nasty smells. There was so much noise and no room to run and play. Maybe it wouldn't matter if I never got a chance to grow up. If I stayed there much longer, I wouldn't survive anyway, let alone grow. I kept wondering what would become of me when we were done coming to this awful place. I knew Carmen, the bad woman, wouldn't let me stay in the little room much longer.

"Lucky, did you hear Carmen tell Cathy about the new horses that are coming to the stable soon? She said if we aren't adopted, we'll need to go to auction. I'm scared. Auction will be worse than this is now. I won't survive auction."

He didn't answer me. He just looked at me with pity.

Oh, just let it stop. Let it be over, please. I didn't want to go into the hot trailer again. So far, during the four months of my life, I'd been in a trailer seven times. When we left there that night, I'd have to go at least once more.

"Lucky, did you hear the women say this is the last day of the fair? They think they may have new homes for most of us. Lucky, you've been adopted, but no one wants me. They're worried. Lucky, did you hear Alice say, 'Maybe if he didn't try to bite people and wasn't so small and thin, someone would want him.'"

No answer. I wanted to yell, "I'm Dinky. I know if I'm loved, I'll be sweet and smart."

It was hard to remember my mother now. She was just a dream in my head. Maybe she didn't honestly tell

me those things. Perhaps, it was as Lucky always said—
wishful thinking. Her voice and smell were so hazy
now. Would someone want me, as they wanted Lucky
and Kaylee? "Please, let someone want me," I
whispered.

Nine

The Meeting

Suffering in silence,
Too young to understand
What the humans have planned.

It was getting close to what used to be our regular dinner time. I saw two humans walking toward us. They smelled of horses and sweat. Obviously the female wasn't enjoying the heat, I thought. Her face was red and sweat dripped from her hair. Still she said, "Ken, let's go look at the babies."

Groaning to myself, I hoped these people wouldn't be more gawkers. Sure, they smelled lovely. But so did the women who nurtured us and then brought us to this dreadful place—the very same sweet smelling women that now forced us to stand all day on display in this hot sun.

Ken and the woman came close enough for me to see the sweat on their brows. They smelled of strange horses. When she put out her hand to let me sniff it, I pinned my ears back and tried to bite her. I had no interest in meeting someone or being fooled again by sweet gestures. She moved her hand back and stood gazing into my eyes. Was she trying to understand me and read my thoughts? Could this woman speak horse?

Doris and Abigail came out of the tent; they were the women on duty this afternoon. They looked at us and turned to Ken. "He's just crabby, hot, and tired of people poking him."

Ken asked them about us. His female continued to gaze at me with a quiet look in her eyes.

Abigail said, "There have been many small children with their parents who have come by the last few days. The children do have a tendency to want to poke and pet the foals. These little ones aren't used to the loud screaming of children."

For a moment, I saw the new woman's look change to one of anger and outrage. Then, turning to me with a smile, her quiet voice said, "I'd be crabby too if I had to stand out here all day in the sun with people poking and staring at me."

Maybe this woman was different. Nervously I stuck my head through the bars of the cage to get a better sniff of her scent. I sensed no fear in her. Even when I nipped, she stood still. Sticking my nose out to sniff her again, she bent down and let me kiss her.

Something was unmistakably different about this woman. I liked her. Standing together nose to nose, sharing our thoughts, feelings, and melding, I hoped, prayed, and wondered, will they adopt me?

All too soon, she moved away and went into the tent. Standing as close to the tent as possible, I listened extremely hard. I wondered if they were asking about me. I heard Doris say, 'Coal,' a couple of times. Then nothing but the murmur of voices came from the tent. Maybe I'd be fortunate too and not have to go to auction or some worse fate.

The little we heard about auction from the other horses as we traveled to and from the fair wasn't good. Auction sounded more horrible than these last three days had been. I couldn't believe anything could be worse. But the horses who'd been there said it was even more humiliating, and they were the lucky ones. They were bought by someone who wanted a horse and not sold for the meat market.

Ken continued to ask questions about the adoption process. He asked where we came from, our names, and many other questions that I didn't understand. Sooner than I expected, they came out of the tent. The woman came back over to me. She seemed not to notice Lucky, even when he tried to get her attention. This surprised me. Everyone always seemed to approve of Lucky. He wasn't scruffy and skinny like me.

She talked sweetly to me again and called me, "little one." She told me I was beautiful and gave me pets and kisses.

Then all too soon, she left. Would I ever see her again? Probably not. Too many disappointments had filled my life. I didn't want to hope too much. I watched as they walked away and heard Ken call her Marta. It was a delightful name. If I were blessed and they adopted me, maybe I could call her Mom or Marta too. As they walked off, I saw her turn around and look at me again. I felt happy for the first time in days. As our gazes met once more, hope arose in me.

All too soon, my optimism left me. We were still there, the day was intolerably hot, and it was past our suppertime. Finally the music stopped. Now Lucky and I watched as people backed trailers up to load animals. Trucks were parked near the booths, and all we heard now was the clank, clatter, and booming sounds of people packing up. The air was thick with the smell of diesel oil and gasoline as trailers were pulled closer. We watched as they led us to the trailer; we could see people scurrying to pull down tents, displays, and all the rides. It was possible this was the last day. Maybe this torture was over. The trailer was hot that morning, but with us all packed so close together, the air felt as if it was on fire. It was scorching our lungs; the humidity made the air almost visible.

Lucky and I waited for the big horses to be loaded. Time seemed to stand still. Finally even the older horses were on the trailer. Yet still we stood there waiting in the heat for the women to begin moving the truck. Listening to the noises around us, we all feared once more.

Would we go home again, like we had the last two days, or go someplace else? Yes, that day was different. The women did pack up everything before we drove off, but our trust was gone.

Where were they taking us now? The big horses told us to be quiet, "We're going home."

But I could smell their fear. Were we going home or had we all been sold to the meat market? We waited while the women loaded the tent and fencing, and listened to them talk about how well the day went. By the time we heard the doors of the truck close, we were drenched with sweat. The waiting was over. The truck finally began to move over the rough ground of the fair. Jostled around inside, Lucky and I tried not to fall or get hurt. The truck drove over the bumpy fairgrounds and onto the smoother road. A short trip, we weren't going to auction or the meat factory. We were going home to our little room for supper and finally a nap.

In our stalls, away from the noise and crowds, eating our supper, I asked, "Lucky, do you think we'll have to go there tomorrow as we have the last three days?"

When he continued eating and didn't answer me, I knew we both were hoping and praying that we heard the women correctly, and the fair was over.

"Alice," Doris said as the three women walked by our room, "I think most of them will be adopted and have homes."

"Maybe even Coal will be adopted," Abigail piped in. "Nothing firm, but a few people did ask about him. I don't think anyone was quite serious though," she finished sadly.

Hearing the name they called me, my ears poked up until I heard Abigail's last statement. Even though the women cared, they wouldn't keep us together or allow us to live here. We'd find homes or we'd be sold at auction. Our time was running out. "Lucky, did you hear what the women said? I didn't hear my name mentioned as one of those they believe will actually be adopted, did you, Lucky?" I wailed.

He didn't reply—just nipped me to move over. He was tired and hungry and didn't have a response for me—nothing to cheer me up or help me get over my fear.

Could humans believe horses felt emotions as they did? Didn't they know we felt fear, apprehension and worry too? Didn't they know a horse could understand their words and wonder about some of the things they said and how they'd apply to them?

Ten

Adopted

What will fate have in store
For the young foal before
He is alone once more?

The day was cooler. Some nice people came to take
Lucky and me out for a walk and to eat the sweet grass.
Lucky was constantly being petted. Why didn't these
people care to pet me too? I wondered as I ate the grass.
Was there something wrong with me? Why didn't
anyone want me? I thought that Lucky was adopted and
was pleased for him.

I was terrified. So far no one had come around to
adopt me. Lucky nuzzled me. He was still my friend. I
believed I would die if no one came for me. Always
hungry, skinny, and with a belly full of crawling things,
I was losing hope. Could I continue to exist if no one
wanted me? All I truly remembered about Mother was
that she was nearly white. Perhaps she was wrong and I

wouldn't grow up tall, strong, and beautiful like she told me a lifetime ago. Even the memory of her words and mind pictures, her scent, and the love she had for me was getting dim.

Lucky's new parents came to take us for a walk again. They let us stop now and then to eat the grass. Hearing a noise, I looked up to see Ken and Marta coming toward us. I remembered them from the fair. Did they come to adopt me? Was I to have a chance to get healthy, stop being hungry, and lose the sick feeling inside my belly? Would I have a forever home?

When they reached us, they stopped. Marta and I kissed. I sniffed and nuzzled her, and she petted me. "We're on our way up to adopt Coal," they said to Lucky's new humans.

I stood there for a minute or two in surprise and disbelief. Then I began to nibble my small patch of grass once more. Looking up as they walked away, I saw Marta turn to look back at me, a smile on her face.

We were in our rooms waiting for our supper when they came back. Ken put a halter on me, a rope around my neck, and pulled me out of the stall. He blocked Lucky when he tried to follow us. Even when Lucky banged against the door, they ignored him. We called to each other. Both of us were afraid to be alone. Why were they being so mean? Ken held me in front of the barn, and Marta had one of those cameras that made a clicking noise.

"Ken, that's enough pictures. Let's put him back in his room and not upset him or Lucky any longer. They'll be separated soon enough when we bring him home."

When they came back to say goodbye, we were eating. I put my ears back and said, "Go away, I don't want to leave Lucky again. Can't you see its suppertime?"

They didn't stay long. They just said a few quiet things to me and left.

"Did I scare them away? Does it mean you will have a home, and I will go to auction?" I asked Lucky.

He didn't know. He only said, "Wait and see." Happy to be adopted, he went on, "Maybe my new people will adopt you too. Then we can stay together, go for walks and eat grass."

Being smart, I knew his humans didn't have any interest in me. They only took me for walks so Lucky wouldn't be scared and cause a commotion.

Days went by. After breakfast, we'd go out to our little field. Every evening we went for lessons. Only now Lucky's new family was learning with him, and I was still with the women. Probably Ken and Marta didn't adopt me. They didn't show up for lessons. Each night I asked Lucky his opinion. He just looked at me sadly and turned back to his food.

A truck pulled up outside our field. It was Marta with a strange man I'd never seen before. "This is Uncle Bob, Coal," she said as she put the halter and rope on me.

Uncle Bob petted me. "He's very cute," he said to Marta. Uncle Bob smelled uncommonly enjoyable. I liked him. He had strange, fun things sticking out of his legs that I could bite and chew on. Then all of a sudden, he picked up my foot and started to mess with it. I didn't like it or the noise of his scraping. I jumped and tried to get away. Marta pushed her body against mine. At the same time, she kept Lucky and Kaylee away from me. Was this adoption? I thought feeling helpless and vulnerable. This wasn't fun like taking walks and eating grass. Where were my walks and treats? Soon Uncle Bob finished messing with my hooves and gave me a hug and pat.

Marta tried to pet me, but I was angry. I wasn't sure I liked her anymore. It seemed she only showed up to

take me away from Lucky. This time she forced me to
stand away from both my friends while Uncle Bob
messed with my feet. Then thinking about auction, I let
her give me a pet goodbye. She smiled at my spirit as
she stood and watched me fight over the only bucket left
with any water in it. Getting water here was sometimes
even harder than getting enough to eat. Whenever I went
over to either the food or the water, Kaylee and Lucky
followed and tried to push me out so they could drink or
eat first. That day I was just too thirsty and angry. I
managed to fight them both off and drink my fill nearly
emptying the bucket. When I looked up, Uncle Bob and
Marta were gone.

Talking everything over with my friends didn't help
at all. Lucky and Kaylee were truly happy with their
new situations. They both got extra feed, treats, and
walks, and their friends came for lessons. I wasn't so
sure of my luck. So far, all I knew since the fair was
being dragged away from my friends for pictures or
having my hooves played with. No, I wasn't sure
adoption was the right thing for me at all. Ken and
Marta didn't show up for lessons or come take me for
walks with my friends. If they were my forever family,
why didn't they come for the fun things?

Day after day went by much the same. Lucky and Kaylee saw their new families. They went for walks, treats, and lessons. Oh, not every day, but most days Lucky and Kaylee's families came, and still my family didn't appear.

One day the women moved Lucky and me. After that, we shared a room with Kaylee. The stall was next to the one we'd been in for many months and a little bit larger. Unfortunately, with three of us sharing, it was extremely cramped.

I liked Kaylee, but I was terribly unhappy. It would be harder for me to get food with three of us sharing the same bucket. To make matters worse, the hay was quickly spoiled. Kaylee had the squirts, and most of the hay was soon inedible. I was losing ground and always hungry. Lucky and Kaylee looked so much bigger and stronger than me. Their coats and manes were shiny because their humans brushed them regularly. The women looked at me with pity when we were all together. Whenever Kaylee and Lucky's families came, they were taken out of our stall and given extra food. They were both growing, and I was shrinking. I was going to die if things didn't change soon. Where was my new family?

Then one morning when we went outside, we saw a new fence in our field. This fence made our field even smaller, and there were new horses on the other side of it. They had the shelter on their side of the fence, and we had no place to go to get out of the rain. The smaller field made it harder to find room to run too. More and more, it looked like there would soon be no room for me.

"Dinky, wake up," Lucky said. "Look at that truck with the immense gray trailer that just pulled up alongside of our field."

"Lucky, it looks like it is Ken and Marta, but who's with them?" We watched as the three humans walked over to the field.

"I'll go in and put the halter on him. Marta, will you keep the other foals out of the way?" Ken asked as he walked me out of the fence. "Coal, this is your Uncle Terry."

What was about to happen? As Ken led me further from the field, I dug in my hooves. I wasn't ready for anymore change. I didn't want to leave my friends. In a firm but gentle voice he said, "Come on, little buddy. You don't have to be afraid."

I followed him, still unsure. Walking to the trailer, Ken said, "Don't be afraid. We're going home now. You're going to meet your new brother and sister." He continued to talk softly to me, and I followed him into the trailer. When he was with me, I felt happy. He spoke and understood horse.

Then the door closed. It felt just like that morning when I was taken away from my mother. I cried and whinnied. Again no one listened. Why couldn't Lucky go with us? I thought as I stood alone in the trailer.

I heard the truck start up, we drove down the road over some rough ground, and then we stopped. It was a short trip, even shorter than the one to the fair. I thought as I called out to them, "Where are we? I'm afraid."

As the trailer door opened, I saw two powerful horses running across a huge field, yelling, "Who are you?" with excitement in their voices.

Eleven

A New Life

> White horse and painted mare
> Such a wonderful pair
> Welcome to your new home
> Said Connella and Chrome

"Who are you? What is this place?" I yelled at the large white horse and the painted mare standing at the fence watching us. "Can I come into your field and stay with you?"

The white horse answered, "I'm Chrome. I'm head horse in this herd."

"I'm Connella and alpha mare," stated the beautiful painted horse.

Marta went through the gate. She put ropes on both of their halters and walked them to the back of the biggest field I'd ever seen. Ken and Uncle Terry led me nearer the gate to the field.

"Ken," Uncle Terry said, "it's best to keep them separated until they learn each other's scent and he's accepted."

"We borrowed some fencing from our friends to make a little paddock for him inside the field."

"That's a great idea," Uncle Terry said, looking over at the little paddock.

Nervously, I stood desperately wanting to run into the field and join my new friends. No matter how much I struggled, Ken held me back away from the fence until Marta had them both at the far end of the vast field away from the gate. Finally, Ken led me into the field and over to a small barn in the corner of the field. The little building had three gigantic rooms, and he put me in one of them all alone.

He walked away with Uncle Terry. I cried for Lucky, for my mother, and for comfort. I prayed that these big, beautiful horses would like me.

It sounded like thunder as Chrome and Connella ran to my room. Hanging their enormous heads over my wall, we sniffed each other.

"What's your name?" they asked at once.

"My name is Dinky," I said. "Please, let me stay. You seem kind, and I'm not frightened when you're near." How beautiful they were, I thought. "You don't seem hungry or scared like most of the other horses I've met." Chrome seemed huge to me, a white male with a little gray on his legs and nose. He was very handsome with a kind, gentle manner.

"There's nothing to be afraid of here, Dinky," Chrome said gently. "We eat extremely well. Don't we, Connella?"

"It's true, little one. Tell us, Dinky, where is your mother? You're extremely young to be without her."

Connella was so beautiful, I thought. All reddish brown and white, her mane and tail were reddish-gold. Although her manner was gentle and sweet, I sensed a stubborn, no-nonsense streak in her.

"We had a couple of days together before the wicked men took me away from her. They hurt her first. She fell on the ground and couldn't get up for a while. I don't like to think about it," I said.

"Little one," she answered with compassion, "you'll be an excellent horse. We'll help you forget about the past, and we'll be your family now. Don't let it worry you anymore, Dinky. This is your forever home. Here you'll grow up tall and strong."

"You're exceptionally cute, but you need to gain a tad of weight," Chrome added.

"We'll teach you the ways of the herd and you'll learn to love it here," Connella assured me while they both nuzzled me over the wall.

I was so small and could barely see over the walls of the huge room. When they were near, I didn't feel afraid though. Was this what it was like to belong? I wondered. Briefly I looked around smelling the new wood, the hay, and the fresh shavings on the floor. Seeing the bucket full of water and the food dish, I knew if I stayed here, I'd be happy.

"You'll like your new home and family, Dinky," Chrome told me. "We're treated kindly, and our bellies are always full. Marta and Ken talk to us, brush us, and our lessons are fun—not hard. If we're sick, our hurts are tended, and we're calmed."

With a tender look in her eyes, Connella said, "I'm a mare. You'll learn that I lead this herd. I'll show you how to find the best food in the field. Chrome will protect us. Marta and Ken will take care of us and feed us. They teach us how to be part of their world, and we show them how to be horses. You'll have lots of amusing things to do here and will be able to run, play, and grow as large as we are."

Afraid it wouldn't last and I would lose my new family as I had lost so much else in my young life, I asked, "Where will I sleep? I've never been alone, except for two times in the trailers—once when I was taken from my mother and just now, when I was brought here."

They looked at each other and said, "Silly kid, you'll sleep in your room or in the field like we do."

I looked at them. "Who will sleep with me, nuzzle and reassure me?" I got no answer. They just looked at me with sympathy in their eyes.

That afternoon Marta came and led Chrome and Connella away. Ken came into my room, put a lead rope on me, and walked me out of the room and around the corner of the small barn. Marta had Chrome and Connella near the front fence in the distance. At the back fence, inside the field, I saw a smaller paddock. Part of it was under a tree for shade. The other part was in the sun. It appeared to be nearly the size of the little field I'd shared with Kaylee and Lucky. Ken took me into the enclosure, took off the lead rope, and went out closing the gate. Looking over my new surroundings, I saw a large red water tub, not a little bucket like we had at the other field, a bowl of grain, and a pile of hay. It appeared I wouldn't be sharing with anyone, and that made me sad. However, it was apparent that now there would be enough food for me too.

Surveying my new surroundings, I heard Chrome's voice. "Hey, Dinky, have something to eat and drink a little water. It will help settle you down and make you feel much better."

After a while, they both wandered away from the fence grazing on some hay in the big field. Unhappy to be separated from my new friends, I followed Chrome's suggestion and ate and drank.

My mind was spinning with all that had happened. It was all so new, a home, and a huge room that seemed too large for just me. Maybe if I was lucky, Chrome or Connella would share it with me. I hoped so. I didn't actually like the idea of being alone without someone to snuggle with.

Exhausted from all the many emotions of the day, lying in the warm sun, my eyes closed, and sensing Chrome and Connella near, I felt safe. In my dreams, I ran and played with Lucky and Kaylee, and then all of a sudden, they turned into Chrome and Connella. Afraid, I woke, opened my eyes, and looked around just to make sure they were still near and it was real. Even though I was disappointed by the certainty that I'd never see Lucky or Kaylee again, I was happy I finally belonged.

Twelve

New Friends

> How can we survive
> Just the two of us
> No herd to protect
> No friendly faces
> Everything new

Looking at me, Chrome said to Connella, "Skinny little thing, isn't he?"

"He's just a baby," Connella said, giving Chrome a dirty look. "He's cute."

"Yes, I suppose he's cute. He does seem rather needy, and I still say he's a skinny little thing."

"Oh, stop it, Chrome. He's afraid and still a baby," Connella snapped. "Let's tell him about our first days here. Then tell him our stories so he can get to know us and not be so scared. Maybe then he'll feel more at home."

"Dinky," Chrome said, "The day Connella and I were put into the trailer by Uncle Terry, we were terribly nervous. Ken and Marta hadn't been around Uncle Terry's for a while. We felt abandoned on that drive, afraid we were going to auction again.

Even though when we arrived Marta and Ken were here, we were still anxious. We missed our buddies back at the old stable. This field felt so huge and empty without them. Neither of us had ever been in charge of protecting the herd, having both spent most of our lives surrounded by other horses. Wherever we lived there was always another horse near us who was alpha mare or male."

"How did you manage, Chrome?" I asked.

"It was hard at first. You see, at Uncle Terry's we were in different fields with different friends. Those first few days here were frightening. We didn't know each other terribly well. The noise of the traffic and the strangeness of the field just added to our alarm."

"The traffic doesn't bother me. I'm used to it. The field is very large though."

"It is indeed," Chrome agreed. "At the other barn there were many horses, and there were fences between us and the road. Here the woods are behind us. There are owls and many other creatures we'd never seen before. It wasn't till we became more comfortable in our new surroundings and with each other that we began to have fun. I had to learn how to be the alpha male for the first time in my life, and Connella became head mare. And we learned to share."

"Kaylee, Lucky, and I shared at our barn," I piped in.

"It's beneficial to have someone to share with, Dinky. Horses are meant to be together," Chrome continued. "Sharing is different when you're young though. When you grow up, you learn your place in the scheme of things and which horse is in charge. Humans have a tendency to change their minds, and what is suitable for them isn't always favorable for us horses."

"Chrome, is it ever true that what's good for us horses is also good for humans?" I asked.

"That depends on the human I suppose, Dinky. Horses have a difficult life in many ways, never knowing if someday we'll be put up for auction. Maybe we'll be sold to someone else or found useless and end up as someone's dinner. Unless you're lucky and find a forever home, life is always uncertain. Sometimes even when you think you're safe, things change. Many humans don't consider that we have feelings too. They may love us, treat us kindly, and find joy in being with us, but if their needs change, we're the first to go."

"Chrome, we have Ken, Marta, and each other," Connella interrupted. "We have love and enough to eat, and we have a lot of room to run and play. We don't have to fight for our food or be lower in the herd anymore. We're king and queen in our own kingdom."

"Of course we have, Connella. Remember how much trouble that first year was? Let me tell you, the weather just wasn't on our side that spring."

"Was it very hot like this summer?" I asked.

"Not really, Dinky. It rained instead. So much in fact, we felt cursed. It rained for weeks. Chrome and I wondered, is it raining at the old stable too, or is it only raining here? As the rain continued to fall day after day, we wondered if we would like it here after all. Every day for weeks on end, it rained. Our big field became a greasy mud pit. Even the grass was trampled into the ground leaving only mud in its place. We couldn't run and play, many of the birds weren't around much, and the dragonflies were totally gone. Even the little cowbirds didn't come around, and it seemed an empty world. With only the rain and gray skies, there was little to keep us occupied. With all the rain, when we tried to walk in the field, the mud came up over our hooves. I think it was nearly two months before it finally dried out."

"That sounds horrible, Connella." I tried to imagine it.

"It was, Dinky. Ken was at work a lot. Lucky for us, Marta was here. She petted and talked to us. All the projects around the farm stopped. Our barn stood half built. It wasn't even a full run-in shelter yet. It had a large blue tarp for a roof."

"At the old field, we had a blue tarp for a roof too," I interrupted. "At least we did until they put a fence up and made it into two fields instead of one."

"Did you have trees to stand under, Dinky, like we do here? Horses in the wild use trees in the rain."

"There were trees, but they were too far away to stand under."

"Did you have to stand in the rain then?"

"I moved here before I found out what would happen in the rain. Did you and Chrome stand under the trees like wild horses, Connella?"

"Chrome and I had never lived in the wild. So in order to keep out of the rain, we spent most of the time standing under the tarp."

"At least they kept it clean, even during the rain."
Chrome interjected.

"Chrome gets terribly antsy with boredom and finds
things to scare us. Yes, Dinky, even adult horses like to
be scared now and then."

I looked at them both with astonishment.

"When the wind blew, the tarp would move. It hung
lower and lower as it filled with water, and it would
slosh over our heads. I hated that," Chrome added.

"Chrome hates tarps, Dinky, especially blue ones.
Yes, it would slosh until Ken or Marta took a large stick
and poked the tarp up, allowing the water to run off onto
the ground behind the barn. Before they did that and it
was sloshing, he'd stand in the rain rather than under the
tarp."

"That's funny." I said smiling.

"It really was, Dinky." Connella answered.

"It wasn't funny to me," Chrome objected.

"Sorry, Chrome, I know you're taller than I am, so
it was natural for you to be more nervous under those
circumstances. After all, the water was much closer to
your head than mine. I suppose I shouldn't make fun,"
Connella said sweetly. "When Marta and Ken talked
about the rain, we heard them say they'd never seen

such a long period of rain either. It was obvious they felt extremely sorry for us. Well, one night they took us into the big red garage. We didn't like the garage much, but at least it was dry, even though the concrete was hard. But at least our food and feet were dry. Finally the rain stopped."

"Don't get the wrong impression, Dinky," Chrome said. "Horses love mud, even us older horses. It's fun to roll in. It keeps the bugs off of us and cools us in the summer. But there's a limit to the amount of mud we like. It's great when it's just enough to roll in, but when it gets deep, then you have to be extremely careful. You cannot run, play, or roll, but must watch your step. I even saw Marta lose her shoe in the mud one day. It was quite funny, watching her walk around in her socks, mud squishing over the tops."

"Her shoes aren't made out of horse hides, are they, Chrome?" I asked.

"No, I don't think so, Dinky," he said before he continued. "Connella and I truly learned to play together when the field dried out. Because she's shorter than my old friend, Rocky, she always got the best of me, until I learned the correct distance to stay away from her when we played. You see, Dinky, one of the things you need to learn when playing is the correct distance to be or a flying hoof will catch you unaware and cause bruising or cuts. Once I got a really deep cut under my chin from playing. Uncle Kris was called to stitch me up. Marta spent many days washing and putting new bandages on me. It was no fun at all. I guess Connella is right, Dinky. Sometimes I can be a bit clumsy."

"We all can, Chrome. I just like to tease you," Connella said making peace.

Chrome gave her a soft look and went on, "Matt, the carpenter, came back to finish the work on the little red house when the rains stopped, and life got extremely entertaining again. Connella liked to watch the giant trucks and earth movers coming and going. They seemed to be everywhere, moving across the front yard, over the driveway, and in back of the house on the hill. See those gigantic rocks? They came out of a hole that the earth movers dug."

"I know what a truck is, but what's an earth mover, Chrome?"

"Dinky, earth movers are immensely powerful; you see the tractor over there? Well, earth movers look a little bit like that, only they're a hundred times bigger."

"A hundred times bigger?" I was amazed.

Chrome continued, "The sound of the saws and the nail guns hurt my ears, but it was fun to watch the trucks. It wasn't long before Connella and I could go to the corner of the barn and see the lights in the house through the new back door. Our barn wasn't like it is now, Dinky, but we had a place to get in out of the sun and rain. We didn't have separate places to eat then. It was all one oversized room. So usually one of us ate inside and the other outside."

"Oh, Chrome, remember the old man that showed up and yelled at Marta? It was shortly after that, Uncle Matt put up the divider between our rooms, and the blue tarp was replaced with a roof."

"Yes, Connella, I remember. They were good days, weren't they? We spent a lot of time learning about each other, our new home, and family. We explored everything and learned the habits of our neighbors. I bet someday they'll start building again, Dinky, and you'll see all the earth movers too."

"I hope so, Chrome. That would be wonderful."

"Even after the divider was up and we had separate rooms, we didn't have doors the way we do now. Instead of doors to keep us in, there were ropes. Marta got very angry with you, Connella, because you wouldn't wait for the rope to be untied before coming out of your stall."

"It was fun though, Chrome. I hated waiting and being stuck in the stall. It was very funny to watch you stand there, when I had free run of the field."

"Still, slipping in and out under the rope was a dirty trick. You see, Dinky, I'm taller than Connella, so I couldn't go under the rope as she did. It made me so crazy to watch Connella get all the best hay."

"It's kind of making me crazy to be locked in here when you two have the run of the field, so I think I understand how you felt, Chrome," I empathized.

"Stop belly aching, Chrome," Connella told him. "It's over now. If we're in our rooms, I have to wait too now. Besides, we both go for walks and we eat the grass. Maybe when you get used to it here, Dinky, and learn the ways of our herd, they'll take you for a walk too."

"I like going for walks and eating the sweet grass."

She continued on as if I never said a word. "They're so busy, between working and building, that we don't get worked that often. It's a vacation full of running, jumping, and eating without a care in the world. Once in a while, one or the other of them will take us into the round pen and either work or ride us."

"What is work and riding, Connella?" I asked.

"Riding is when one of the humans gets on our back and we carry them, Dinky."

"Aren't they heavy?"

"Not really, you get used to it when you're bigger." Chrome replied.

"Back then, the round pen was in our paddock, not behind the fence as it is now. I guess I wasn't sympathetic to Chrome when he was being worked in the round pen. I'd run around outside and stir him up. It really distracted him and made Marta awfully angry," Connella confessed.

"Dinky, just wait until you see the cyclist that rides the strange bicycle. He lays down on it. His clothes and the bicycle are both bright yellow. It's very funny to watch him going down the street, and Connella and I always run to the fence for a real close look when he goes by."

"It's our job to watch out for our neighbors, Dinky. Besides, they do intriguing things, so it's also fun," Connella added. "Chrome, why don't we tell him about our past? Maybe then he'll feel comfortable telling us about his."

hirteen

Chrome

Once it was different
But now my name's Chrome,
And this is my home.

"Why don't you go first Chrome?" Connella said.

"Okay, Connella, I'll start my story before I met Marta. My first humans named me Ash Ka Nam—what a mouth full," he said laughing. "I used to be small like you, Dinky, though not so skinny. I thought I would always live with the herd where my mom raised me. But one day a trailer came and took me away. It was a long time before I understood why my family decided they no longer wanted me."

"Did they take you away from your mom too, Chrome? I asked.

"Not really, Dinky. By then, my mother and I lived in different fields. I shared a field with my buddy, before he was hurt in a race and had to be put down. I was still mourning him deeply, when a day or two later I was sent to auction. That's why they sent me away. They no longer needed me to be a companion to their race horse."

"What's auction like, Chrome? Is it like the bad stories I've heard?"

"Auction is terrible, worse than you probably heard. Mine started off with a horrible ride. At night they took me out of the trailer to clean it and feed me. At auction they put me into a corral packed with a bunch of other horses. We were all frightened standing and waiting for our turn on the block. You could smell the fear and sweat in that corral. Every one of us was silent and restless with fear. When it was my turn, I heard a man talking extremely fast. I didn't know what he was saying, until l heard him say, 'Going, going, gone,' and I knew I'd been sold. After that, I was led to a crowded paddock till the end of the day. I didn't know my destiny yet.

"It was nearly dark when I was put in another trailer with a few other horses. All of us were fearful of our fate during the miles we drove before we finally stopped. Luckily, we found ourselves at the stable where we were to live for a while. We were the fortunate ones not destined for the meat market. There'd be a chance for us live.

"You see, Dinky, I'd heard the horror stories from the others in the crowded corral at auction. Some of the people bidding only wanted us for meat or hides. At the end of the auction, there were a group of horses that hadn't been sold. Those horses were sold by lot and usually ended up at the meat markets or the tanners. Oh, I knew that the other horses didn't have any first-hand information or experience, yet the fear was prevalent. They'd seen horses at other auctions sold in lots. I was unbelievably happy when I saw the barn and the herds of horses and ponies at my new home.

"When I first arrived there, they put me in a small enclosure with a herd of ponies. You see, I tended to lose weight quickly and was extremely skinny. It was embarrassing, but at least I now got enough to eat. Many weeks later, Uncle Terry thought I'd gained enough weight, and they put me out in the field with the big hack herd."

"What's a hack herd, Chrome?"

"Well, Dinky, hack horses have to earn their keep. They're used for trail rides and lessons. They aren't owned by one person and don't have a family like we do."

"That sounds horrible, Chrome."

"Well, I can tell you, it wasn't much fun. One day I overheard Uncle Terry say to Aunt Becky, 'It's time Chrome began to earn his keep.'

"She replied, 'He'll make a fine lesson and trail horse, Terry.' From then on I worked long days, especially in the summer. It wasn't a fun life. There was a lot of work and not enough food—at least I didn't think there was. It seemed I was always hungry. There always seemed to be some human who didn't know how to ride on my back or pulling at my mouth day after day. Even though at the stable they didn't work us for terribly long hours, it seemed like a long time when you didn't care much for the work.

"Because I was fighting for my share of hay in the field, I began to drop weight again. You see, Dinky, I'm a thoroughbred and what humans call a hard keep. I was quite unused to being in a herd with so many horses.

"Where I grew up, at first it was just me and my mom. Then I played and romped with the other foals. When I grew older, they began to train me to be a race horse."

"Did you race?" I asked.

"No," he told me, "I never raced. I was the companion horse for my buddy, who was a race horse. We lived and trained together. On race days, I would walk to the gate with him, give him words of encouragement, and keep him calm. He was my best friend, and I still miss him. It's been years now since we were together, and sometimes I do have trouble remembering his scent. He was my friend—I remember that. We shared a field, just the two of us, and never had to fight over food. You see, they needed him to be in prime condition for the races, so we were well fed. Then one day, he broke his leg racing. Right there on the field I watched as they put him down. It was awful, Dinky. I'm glad they never raced me," Chrome said sadly.

"He died?" I asked.

"Yes, he did, Dinky, and it was very sad." Chrome said before going on. "Uncle Terry's farm had some nice horses. I picked my friends carefully and quickly became part of a small group within the herd. As for the others, I stayed out of their way. The life was hard and sometimes depressing. Some of the people who came to ride weren't as pleasant as Aunt Becky and Uncle Terry were.

"Most days I'd be out on the trail or in the training ring. Because I was large and gentle, most of the time my riders would be humans who feared horses. Still I was happy enough, except for being hungry all the time. I couldn't seem to get enough to eat. In a large herd, there's always a horse higher in rank than you are. Sometimes the alpha horse would push me away from the pile of hay I was eating."

"I know what that's like, Chrome. Lucky always pushed me away so he could eat extra."

Chrome looked at me with pity, and then continued his story. "Before I met Marta, I'd lost about two-hundred pounds. We thoroughbreds lose weight quickly. One day it's there and then next it's gone; it makes it hard for humans to notice we're losing it right away. Uncle Terry and Aunt Becky noticed my weight loss quickly though and began bringing me in for breakfast and supper. Soon my belly felt much better."

"I hope my belly feels better soon."

"I promise you, your belly will feel better, Dinky." Connella interjected.

I smiled at Connella and then asked Chrome, "When did you meet Marta?"

"Well, Dinky, with Marta and me, it was love at first sight. The evening we met started out the same as every evening. I was brought in, put in someone else's room and given some hay. We hack horses didn't have stalls. As it wasn't dinner time, I knew that this meant more work. I'd be put on the cross ties and gotten ready for either a trail ride with some stranger or a lesson in the ring with one of the students.

"Then it happened. She walked into the stable and stopped at each stall visiting with a kind word and a pet for the horse or pony in every room. When she got to me, she petted me and talked kindly to me. She's small with dark eyes, a warm smile, and a gentle touch. It felt as if she knew what I was thinking. Ah, I see you've experienced the same thing with Marta."

"Yes, I felt it too the moment she looked at me."

"I could tell by your look, youngling. All too soon, I heard and saw Aunt Becky walk in and say 'Hi Marta.' That's when I first heard her name. She turned around, her back to me, and spoke to Aunt Becky. I didn't want her to stop talking to me. I knew she was my human, so I wrapped my head around her, the way we horses hug a human. With a happy laugh, she began petting me again. That night we had our first lesson together. After that, I saw her once a week when she came for a lesson or a trail ride. Marta smelled sweet like Auntie Becky, and both have kind hearts."

"Will I meet Aunt Becky?"

"I am sure you will, Dinky. You'll like her, she speaks horse too," Connella said kindly. "Go on with your story, Chrome."

"Okay, Connella. One day she didn't come to see me first when she got to the stable. This was unusual for her. I'd always been her first stop. I heard her car and her voice, but she didn't come into the barn. I was in the stall for a long time before she finally came down. Something was different. Her excitement was palpable. She whispered to me, 'You're my horse now.' Dinky, it was one of the happiest moments of my life."

Mesmerized, I listened. I knew what Chrome meant when he talked about finding out you belonged. Staring into his soft brown eyes, I waited.

"For a while, I was confused. Instead of having my own room, and living in the boarder's field, I stayed out in the hack field. Even my friends made fun of me. They didn't believe I had a human of my own. I was still being used as a lesson horse or had some stranger on my back on the trail. I didn't understand either, and I was embarrassed. I couldn't even explain it to myself. How could I tell my buddies? How I could be her horse and still be a work horse like the other hack horses?

"Finally she explained, 'Chrome while I finish paying your adoption fee, I need you to help with the room and board by letting other people ride you for lessons and trail rides. Once I finish paying for your adoption, you won't have to worry about the other people riding you anymore.'

"I was so proud, I pranced around the field when we had our lessons, and held my head high. I knew I had met my forever friend. We'd be a real family. She told me one day she'd have a house. I'd come live with her and Ken and not live at the barn with the other horses. A few days later, she had Uncle Kris look at the tattoo in my mouth."

"You have a tattoo in your mouth, Chrome? What's a tattoo?" I asked.

"A tattoo is a way humans put a mark on a horse that gives its lineage."

"What's lineage?"

"I'm not sure, Dinky. I only know that the next day, Marta put her hand on my head, and I saw a picture of my mother and me when I was a baby. It was a very special moment, I can tell you. I was certain she could speak horse after that. The only thing I hate is the days she gives me a bath. I love the coolness of the water on the hot days after she takes the saddle off of me. I don't like having my face washed though, and she always insists on doing it anyway.

"It wasn't long after that when Uncle Terry took me from the hack field and put me out in the boarder's field. The boarder's field didn't have as many horses in it as the hack field.

"It was obvious to me that Aunt Becky's horse, Zepher, was the alpha male in this field. So I minded my manners and paid him respect. Dinky, it's crucial to know your place in the herd, or things go terribly hard on you. When dinner time came, I knew which room was mine without being told and happily went into it for my supper.

"One day, I overheard Marta tell the last of the women who'd been riding me, 'Sally, you won't be riding Chrome anymore.' Sally got terribly angry and said many terrible things about Marta to some of the other women, but I was glad she wouldn't be riding me anymore. Sally's hand was heavy on the reins, and she made me run on the paved roads when Marta wasn't around. 'Chrome will be moving to our home soon, so I want him to get used to it just being us,' Marta told Sally. Then I knew for sure I had a forever family, and my days as a hack horse were finally over."

"When did you and Connella meet, Chrome?"

"It was only a short time later when we met, Dinky. At first, we didn't like each other much. The day Ken brought her in to eat in the stall next to my room, we said many harsh words to each other. She was decidedly distrustful of me at first. You see, Dinky, Connella had been in a small field with a truly dominating male for many years, but I'll let her tell you that story."

 *Fourteen*

Connella

> I am mare proud and brave
> Beautiful but no slave
> Respect me, I don't bend
> Unless you are my friend

"Dinky, my name is Connella. Although, he's a thoroughbred and I'm a quarter-horse, my bloodline is as rich as Chrome's. Nevertheless, we both faced the auction block. I quickly discovered that the woman who'd bought me, the one I thought would be my forever friend wasn't interested in getting to know me."

"Is that like the nice women at the barn who rescued me, and then took me to the fair?" I asked.

"It's probably similar, Dinky. In her own way, she was good to me. I had my own stall and shared a tiny space in a field about the size you described yours was with a male horse. In our field there was no grass, not even weeds, just dirt, except in the rainy season. Then it was mud. At least we had plenty of water and food. We had our own dishes, whether we were in our stalls or out in our little field.

"My male was extremely demanding and domineering. He was always pushing me around and wouldn't allow me to speak to any of the other horses over the fence. He was the jealous sort, as many males are, not gentle and kind as Chrome is. The woman who bought me would bring us a sweet feed. It was tasty, but made me fat. I had too much energy and not enough room to run, so I became exceedingly lazy and didn't want to move around much.

"She was nice and came every day to feed us. Once in a while, she'd brush me, saddle me, get up on my back, and just want me to run. Unfortunately, she didn't give me the time to warm up my muscles or get to know her. I began to think of her as my meal ticket. One day I found out that if I bucked when she tried to get me to run, she would fall off, and the ride would end. I think she became afraid of me."

"What is bucking, Connella?" I asked.

"It's probably not something that you should even think of doing with a human on your back, Dinky. You will, however, learn it as your muscles develop."

Chrome spoke up, "Go on, Connella."

"I didn't mind that she didn't want to ride me. Who wants someone on your back if they don't know you and you don't respect them? In a way I guess it was my fault that one day she gave me away to Uncle Terry, and I was in the hack field.

"My male and I had been together a long time, and even though he was bossy, demanding, and jealous, it hurt to be separated. To lose all you know in the space of a few minutes, does leave you bewildered and upset. You must be feeling a bit afraid and puzzled right now, Dinky."

"I've been scared and confused for a long time, Connella."

"It will get better, my little friend. You'll see—this will be an excellent change," Connella said before going on with her story.

"Those first few days apart were spent hanging around his field. We mourned over the fence, and he tried to break through it a few times. One day he managed to break through the fence. After that he was put in his stall, and we couldn't talk or comfort each other anymore. My room was given to a small black Arabian. I lived out in the hack field no matter the weather. I no longer had my own room, nor was I brought in for supper."

"You didn't get supper anymore?" Astonished, I said.

"I got hay, but no grain, Dinky, and after many weeks of having the horses in the hack field chase me away from the food, I decided it just wasn't worth trying to fit in with the big herd. Besides I was tired of fighting. I stayed away from the head mare and the males and picked one little friend to protect. Her name was Nellie. She was a Halfling."

"What's a Halfling, Connella?"

"A Halfling is part horse and part pony." Connella went on, "She had a sweet nature, and she didn't mind taking second place to me. We were staunch friends, Nellie and me.

"Once I was in the hack field, Ken and Marta would visit me more regularly. They brought us treats. Ken would spend time talking to me and telling me stories. He called me 'pretty girl' and 'baby girl.' At the same time, I had another human friend, a young girl who would take me from the field and brush me. One day my hoof began to hurt. She spent weeks soaking it, which made it feel much better. She was exceptionally kind to me, and I knew she loved me.

"Unfortunately, she was a bit afraid of me. I could tell when she'd take me out for a ride or try to work me a bit in the ring. I think she was afraid I would buck her off, the way I did the other woman. I liked her a lot, but she wasn't strong enough, so I pushed her around. And if I didn't want to do something, well I just wouldn't."

Interrupting, Chrome said, "You truly can be remarkably stubborn, Connella. You still have much to learn about humans."

"Shut up, Chrome. I know I'm not perfect, but this is my story. Why should I work hard for some human that doesn't take the time to know me or spend time with me and obviously isn't either an alpha mare or alpha male? You tell me that, Chrome. Now be quiet, and let me finish my story."

Astonished, my little head went back and forth as I listened to the two of them argue. I didn't know that grown up horses had arguments.

"One day Ken came out to the field. Nellie and I went over to say hello. We thought we might get some pets and treats. Instead, Ken put a rope around my neck and took me out of the field. I was very surprised. This was the first time he'd ever done more than pet me or give me treats. I knew he was a decider, and I liked him a lot, so I went calmly into the barn with him. I was happy even though I did feel sad for poor Nellie, left alone with no one to look after her while I was gone.

"After bringing me out of the field, he put me in a stall, gave me some grain, and brushed me. We were all alone in the barn until Marta came in with Chrome and put him in the stall next to me. I looked at this big, white, goofy male and took an instant dislike to him. Dinky, don't get me wrong, Chrome is large, beautiful, kind, and strong, but he does have a goofy side to him. I think it's the Minnesota farm boy in him. I didn't want him to think he could push me around as all the other males tried to do, so I put my ears back and gave him what for.

"You see, we knew things were changing. While Ken brushed and talked to me, Marta was in Chrome's stall brushing and talking to him. Chrome and I quickly figured out we would be forced to be mates. It was apparent Chrome liked the idea. He had never had a mate. I, for one, didn't care to have another gelding try to lord things over me or push me around. I'd already had too much of that. Besides, I already knew Ken was

alpha male, so where did Chrome fit into the picture? He
was only a lower male. I was determined to have
nothing to do with him. I'd spent about two years at this
stable, and I didn't honestly expect to leave it. I didn't
see why I should try to be friends with him when the
only time we would see each other was when Ken and
Marta came to the stable together."

"You really were quite difficult, Connella."

"Chrome, I told you to be quiet. I didn't interrupt
you when you were telling your story. Please don't
interrupt me." Putting her ears back, Connella had
certainly told Chrome off.

Hardly able to peek over the top of the door, I
looked on in wonder. It still surprised me to see grown-
ups argue just like foals.

Connella went on with her story. "Ken would take
lessons with me and Aunt Becky. I loved him. Though I
knew he wasn't a proper rider, he would learn. He kept
looking down at me. I think it was because he loved me
and took pleasure in looking at me, not realizing it threw
me off balance. Because I loved and respected him, I
decided to help him. I stopped and waited till he righted
himself. I wasn't going to throw him off the way I did
the others. The connection between us was strong.

"One day I overheard Aunt Becky ask Ken if he minded going for a trail ride instead of having a lesson. What an incredible adventure we would have. It had been a long time since I was out on the trails. Even though I wasn't sure Ken was ready, I was quite happy. I loved the idea of riding the trails, and I hated the ring, even though I loved the attention from Ken. What I didn't know was that Chrome and Marta would be going too."

"What are trails, Connella?"

"They're paths through the woods or across fields, Dinky. It's great fun. Sometimes there are hills to go up and down or streams to wade through."

"Do you think I'll ever go on trails, Connella?"

"Probably, Dinky," Connella replied patiently before continuing her story. "After we were saddled up, off we went with Aunt Becky in the lead on Zepher. After her came Marta on Chrome, Uncle Lee on Fancy, and Ken and I brought up the rear. Things were going well. We were all just out for a Sunday stroll. The weather was beautiful, not too hot, with a delightful breeze blowing. Sometimes Ken and I would hang back a little and then run or trot to catch up. It was a wonderful time, and I knew Ken was happy too. Shortly into our adventure, Marta asked Aunt Becky if she and Chrome could lead for a while.

"It was awful. Chrome would take one step, stop, and look around. He'd look back at us and ask us if we were all okay, and if we were all still with him. Goodness, it was funny. After all, where would we go? If he continued like this for the whole ride, it would be dark before we got back to the barn, and I'd miss my supper. Even though we could tell he felt the responsibility keenly, it was a joke."

Chrome interrupted again, "It wasn't THAT awful. I just wasn't used to Marta and me being in charge. It had always been Aunt Becky on trail rides."

"Chrome, please, this is my story," Connella repeated.

My eyes were round with wonder at the pictures that formed in my head. I was amazed that a great horse like Chrome could act so silly. "More please, Connella," I begged.

"Later after the ride, Chrome and I were in adjoining stalls again having a little grain. I turned to him and asked, 'Chrome, do you know what's happening? Things just keep changing.'

"He told me he'd overheard Marta and Ken talk about moving us to their house to live with them. We didn't quite understand what that meant. Were they going to share stalls with us? It was only a few weeks later that we found out.

"Dinky, when you move from an extremely large horse farm, and suddenly you're all alone with a near stranger in a new field noisy with traffic, you're afraid. You must remember, Dinky, Marta and Ken are the deciders in this herd. After them, it's Chrome and me. You must learn your place too. If you don't learn your place things can go hard on you. You can be sent to Coventry, Dinky."

"Where's Coventry? Is it far away? Would I have to ride in a trailer again? I don't like trailers."

"Dinky, Coventry isn't a place you go to; it's a frame of mind. When others don't approve of you or what you are doing, they shun you. It's much the same as being told to go to your stall or off in a corner and think about your actions. It really isn't fun at all, for no one will talk to you or play with you when you are in Coventry."

Fifteen

Stories

When the rain turns to ice
It is not very nice.

I listened breathlessly as they told me their stories. "Please, tell me more about your lives and what it's like here."

"Sure, Dinky, but don't you want to tell us about your life now?" Connella asked.

"No, Connella, I want to forget the hurtful things. I like to hear about what my home will now be like."

"If you're sure, little one, I will go on; though I think someday you will need to talk about it."

I nodded. "Not now, Connella. I want to hear more about it here, please."

"The first winter here was tremendously fun. Much more fun than when we lived at Uncle Terry's. There was so much room to run, play, and roll in the snow, and

127

no one around to stop us or push us around." Connella stated.

"At Uncle Terry's, we had our own friends, but we still had to listen to the head male, even if we didn't like him," Chrome interjected. "In the winter our fur grew really thick to keep us warm, and it wasn't hot and humid like summer time. The bugs would go away to wherever they went in the winter. All we knew was they didn't pester us in the winter."

"Winter is the best time," Connella went on as if Chrome had never opened his mouth. "Except for ice storms—they're terrible. Neither Chrome nor I had ever been through anything like an ice storm before. It rained sleet all evening, and late that night, the rain became ice. As it hit the trees, everything began popping."

"Trees were falling down and erupting everywhere," Chrome explained.

"It was dreadfully cold, dark, and scary," Connella said, ignoring him. "Chrome and I huddled together as far away from the trees and the barn as we could get. We spent our night watching everywhere and jumping at each noise, afraid a tree would hit us. It sounded like a war to us. Have you ever heard gunfire, Dinky?"

"Yes, I did the day the men shot my mom and took me away from her. It was the worst noise I've ever heard. I heard one of the men say to drug her. What does drug mean, Connella?"

Connella looked at me with pity and answered, "I think drugged means to get sleepy. When Uncle Kris is going to do our teeth, Chrome is drugged so he'll stand still."

It was becoming hard for me to keep up with which horse was saying what. Chrome and Connella kept talking over each other. They both wanted to tell me their part of the story, and my head got sore from whipping back and forth listening to one or the other.

"Now and then a tree would fall," Connella continued. "Mostly they exploded. One of them landed on the roof of Marta and Ken's house, another one on their cars, and two more just flew through the air and landed on our fence. We were both freezing with ice hanging off our hides.

We were afraid to go under a tree or in the barn for shelter. Maybe a tree would come down on us or hit the barn. As the night wore on, Marta and Ken would check on us. They came out carrying lights and spoke to us quietly, trying to calm us down. We could sense that they were afraid for us. Near dawn it stopped."

"As soon as it was light enough, we were fed a warm, mushy grain to take the cold from our bones. Our hides were covered with about an inch of ice, so they rubbed us down. It was extremely soothing," Chrome said, talking over Connella.

"Unfortunately," Connella interjected, "before we had a chance to relax and take a nap, the noise of the saws began. To our tired minds, it appeared as if a crowd of men were cutting up trees and pounding nails around us. Our fence was fixed. The trees were taken off of the cars and the roof of the little house.

"Chrome hated the sound of the saw as it ate through the branches cutting the trees into a size that could be moved. He jumped at the sound of the hammer as Uncle Kevin, Uncle Dave, and Ken put the fence back up. It was just too much noise, and we were both still nervous and tired from a night without sleep."

Chrome chimed in, "About noon the sun broke through the clouds. The fence was all repaired. Everyone except for Ken and Marta were gone. We were too tired from the night of terror and didn't enjoy the sun that day; we spent most of it dozing.

"The next few weeks, we didn't see much of Marta. Ken told us she had to work long hours answering calls from people like us who had no power. Connella and I didn't understand what power was till Ken explained it to us. Power is what makes the lights in the field turn on, the water come out of the hose, and it keeps the water free of ice in our trough. Without power, Ken spent a lot of time driving the little tracker around getting water for us from the brook behind the house or chipping the layer of ice off our water."

"At least he talked to us and explained everything," added Connella.

My little head went back and forth as they shared this part of their story. I didn't know what snow or ice was, but ice sounded ghastly. Trembling with dread, I asked the two of them, "What will happen if the ice comes again? How will we stay alive?"

They both were quick to assure me that, in all their lives, it was the only time the ice had come. "It probably will never come again, Dinky," Connella said. "At least Chrome and I hope not, but if it does you'll live, like Chrome and I did. Marta and Ken will reassure us and bring us warm food to heat our bellies. Then the sun will come out again. At least we'd hope so. It's a good life

here, Dinky. Oh look, Chrome is starting to settle down
a bit. He looks a little sleepy."

Sixteen

Coventry

> When you learn, Dinky,
> The fields will be yours.
> Across them you'll fly
> On hooves so swiftly.

Waking from my nap and still a bit groggy from sleep, I yelled, "Where is everyone? I'm afraid. My dreams are full of ice storms. Please, don't leave me alone." Peeking over the wall of my room, I saw Chrome and Connella munching hay. Ken and Marta were still sitting at the table by the fence, and Uncle Terry had left. I was still shut in and didn't like it. "The afternoon sun is warm. Please, come let me out." Ken and Marta got up from the table and walked over to me. "Please, let me play with my friends."

Impatiently, I stood as they put a rope on my halter and led me out of the stall. "No, no, I want to be with my friends," I told them, planting my feet firmly as they tried to lead me into the small enclosure inside the big field. A fence separated me from Chrome and Connella. I'll show you, I'll be with my new friends I thought and jumped over the gate. Marta caught me, fighting every step of the way until she had me back in the enclosure.

"I don't want to stay in here," I yelled, but she ignored me and only held me tighter as Ken fixed the gate, making it too high for me to jump again. Resigned to my fate, I surveyed my surroundings. In one corner stood the oversized red bucket full of fresh water—more water than Lucky, Kaylee, and I had in our little field. On the ground was the large black dish with fresh grain in it and off to the side a new pile of hay. Maybe it wouldn't be so terrible after all, I thought, trying to make the best of everything. We could at least talk over the fence and sniff each other. Watching Chrome and Connella in the big field, I stretched my legs, running up, down, and around my little paddock. Still, I wasn't happy cooped up away from my new friends. I missed playing and nuzzling with Lucky and Kaylee.

"Connella," Chrome said, "it's nearly supper time." Sure enough, Marta and Ken took Chrome and Connella into their rooms for grain. No longer able to see them and feeling alone, I ran and charged the fence, screaming and crying. Finally, they came and led me toward the barn. I could see Chrome and Connella again.

"You sure do make a fuss, Dinky," Chrome commented. "Don't worry. Soon we'll all have our supper."

"Why are we all in different rooms?" I asked them. When they looked at me as if I was crazy, I stopped talking and waited. As they promised, our buckets were soon filled with food. Still puzzled, I asked, "Aren't we going to share a bucket?" Too busy eating they paid no attention. It was the first time in my life I was eating alone, except when the dirty men fed me on the truck. After pushing my food around a bit and looking at it, I ate. I felt better about everything after my belly was full, so I waited. I was surprised. For once I wasn't hungry.

Bewildered again when they put hay in my room and shut the door, I asked Chrome, who was nearest to me, "Why don't you and Connella have hay in your rooms?"

Chrome looked at me strangely, "Dinky, Connella and I will have our hay in the big field. See, they're already putting it out."

Looking over, I saw he was right. There were large stacks of hay in the field near my room. "Why do I have to stay in here?" I asked Marta and Ken as they petted me and said goodnight.

"Poor little thing," Marta said, "I hope he doesn't feel too lonely tonight."

"He'll be safe, and that's what counts," Ken answered her. "Besides, he can still see Chrome and Connella. He won't feel alone."

Putting my ears back, I yelled as they walked away, "You're wrong. I am lonely. Who will snuggle me tonight?"

I looked around the big stall. In the corner was my pile of hay, a full water bucket hung on the wall, fresh shavings lay on the floor, and still I was troubled. I watched Chrome and Connella eat their hay in the field near me. It had been a busy day, and I was tired. Maybe it wouldn't be too distressing, I thought, munching on my hay trying to make the best of things.

I awoke all alone screaming, "I'm scared," crying for Lucky or someone to comfort me. Chrome and Connella came running.

"Shush, little one, we're here," Connella murmured. "Chrome, tell Dinky the story about the Peppermint Gang, please."

"Well, at our old barn the pasture was fenced in with electric wire, Dinky," I heard Chrome telling me quietly as I fell asleep.

Startled again out of sleep by a strange hooting sound, I screamed. Chrome and Connella came over and soothed and nuzzled me, "It's only Sir Owl, Dinky," Connella said. "Don't worry. He won't hurt you. Sir Owl is our friend. He eats snakes, rats, and other rodents."

As the night wore on, it became all too easy to tell my new friends were getting very irritated and tired. The next morning, Chrome put his ears back when he saw me poke my head up over the wall. They both were in a fine snit. He was even crabby with Ken and Marta.

When they came to give us breakfast, Connella put her ears back and her nose between the bars that separated their rooms. Chrome jumped around kicking the walls. I looked on cringing as Marta scolded him and told him to stop. At last, we all had our breakfast. I liked the smell of Chrome's food much better than my own, but I was hungry. Soon all I could hear was the occasional snort and the sound of chewing.

Connella finished first. Waiting impatiently to get out to the hay in the field, she turned to me and said,

"Hurry up, Dinky. We're liable to have to stand here and wait till you're done and they take you out to the little paddock."

I stopped eating and looked at her. "Connella, please, tell me I can come out to the big field today."

"I don't think so, Dinky, and after keeping us up all night, I expect you will be in Coventry today. I don't think you should be around Chrome anyway."

Just as I finished breakfast, Marta came and took me out to the little corral. Again I was separated from Chrome and Connella. With a sad face, I looked around my small paddock. I watched them in the field eating their hay and thought, I'm alone. Even though they had piles of hay near my fence, we were separated. I was smart. I understood when Ken and Marta said, "Dinky, you must all get to know each other before you can go into the big field. We don't want to take the chance that you'll play too hard and get hurt." What I didn't grasp was why they thought my new friends would hurt me. They both seemed remarkably caring and compassionate, and I was eager to be a part of their herd. It wasn't natural for a horse to be alone all the time, I thought, stamping my feet.

The morning sun moved higher in the sky. I began to appreciate the separation, even though I didn't like it. Chrome was angry at me. He charged the small fence whenever I got close enough to try to sniff him or Connella. Chrome had been kind to me the day before, but I knew I was in the dog house for keeping them up all night.

"You must learn," he said to me. "I'm the boss in this herd. We didn't appreciate your antics last night."

"I'm sorry, Chrome. Please don't be mad," I apologized, but it didn't help. "I'll find a way to make it up to you. I promise."

He said nothing as he walked off. I was determined somehow I would make it better, yet each time I tried, he said quite sternly, "Leave it be, little one, I'm tired and you must be trained."

Dusk drew near. It was my second night here, and I was quieter. Holding my head up as high as possible, I could barely see over the walls. It didn't help if I couldn't see them. I was still alone. Missing Lucky, our talks, and nuzzling, I looked around the spacious room and felt sorry for myself.

That day I discovered I mustn't keep Chrome and Connella up all night. They would never admit me into the herd if I didn't learn. It was important to be accepted, to have a place, a home, and a family of my own. If I was to grow tall and strong like Chrome, I needed to learn the ways of the herd.

"Please," I prayed to the horse gods, "help me comprehend quickly." I was so alone and frightened. They would have to accept me, just the same as they did that very first day. What would happen if they decided they didn't like me? Would I be sent away and again lose the chance of a family and love? I was unsure of everything, except that starting tonight, I must be quiet.

I woke to a new day. Maybe today I'd be allowed to be in the big field. I detested being alone, and hearing the humans talk as if they understood my feelings didn't help.

"We must be sure he's secure before letting him into the herd," Marta said. "He's so small and thin. It's obvious that he feels terribly alone, Ken, but we must be sure he's safe. Yesterday didn't go as well as the first day for him."

Quietly walking to the little corral, I felt disheartened by the idea of spending another day alone, only able to watch them play in the big field. Possibly they'd visit with me, I thought, running around my paddock. Hopefully, they'd come and eat the hay that was near my little enclosure. That would help a little, not enough, but a little.

"Am I being weaned? Am I in Coventry?" I asked Connella. She didn't respond. Feeling isolated, I lay down near my water tub to take a nap. I despised being separated, only able to get to know the two of them over the fence or the door of my room. I loathed the separation and seclusion. Oh, sometimes Chrome and Connella would talk to me. Mostly they ignored me, going about their business. Why was I being punished? Why did they bring me here if I wasn't to run in the large field and learn to be a family with my new friends? I hadn't been separated from Lucky and Kaylee when I went to the other stable. Why did I have to be here?

Twilight rolled in, and I stood watching from my little paddock as Chrome and Connella went off to their rooms. Soon I knew I'd be led into my room. There wouldn't even be a chance to run in the big field. I planted my feet in the dirt as Ken put the rope on my halter and cried, "No, I don't want to go into the large room again. It's not natural for me to be alone." Alas, Ken was stronger than me. I was again shut into the stall.

Hay was brought into my room. Peeking over the door and looking around, I saw Chrome and Connella quietly eating the hay in the field. "Why?" I yelled as I put my ears back at Marta. "I don't want to stay in here again. I feel so forlorn. It's worse than the day I was taken away from my mother before I met Lucky. You don't understand. Please, let me out," I begged and looked at her mournfully as she walked away.

I was getting stronger and healthier but sadder. Since Marta gave me the peppermint stuff, the strange crawly feeling left my belly. Chrome and Connella talked about me and the changes that were coming as if I wasn't there. They ran up and down the field having a grand old time, while I could only run in little circles in the small paddock. The big field beckoned.

"Please, tell me when I can come out to play with you and be a family?" I asked them. Once in a while one or the other took pity on me and came to the fence to talk to me for a time. "I want to run and play with you so much. Yes, the room is new and beautiful. I'm glad I don't have to fight for my food, but I hate it. I'm tired of being alone all night."

"Dinky, you aren't by yourself." Connella said.

"Yes, I am, Connella. It's just me and my thoughts all night. The noises are so strange and unfamiliar. I can barely see you and Chrome even if I stretch my neck. It doesn't matter that you're both near. Most nights I feel like it's only me and these walls."

"Dinky, Chrome and I need our time too. We come as often as possible to tell you stories. But we need to move around a bit. We can't play babysitter all night. Tonight we'll tell you the story about snow before you go to sleep."

Their stories made such incredible pictures in my mind. How much fun it would be, I thought, when everything got white. The thought of the snow making the ground fun to run on, roll in, and throw high into the air was amazing. The noise of the traffic muffled by the snow, the air quiet, and the tall white banks growing along the road sounded so magical to me.

"Connella, do you think they'll let me out of the little paddock before winter?"

"We'll see, Dinky, but it will probably be long before winter," Connella reassured me.

Chrome added, "Dinky, Connella likes to play snow plow."

"Connella, what's a snow plow?"

"They're great, hulking, noisy things that go down the street in the winter. They push all the snow off the road. It flies through the air and lands on the sides of the road. Voila! A path for the cars to drive through is made. I love to watch the plows. Sometimes I mimic them by sticking my nose in the snow at one end of the field. Then I'll run the length of it tossing my head back and forth. Just like the plows, the snow flies in the air. When I'm done, we have a path through the field," Connella said.

"Oh that sounds fun. Do you think I can do it too?"

"Maybe when you get a bit bigger, Dinky. I don't think your nose is large enough yet," Connella answered.

I was still a bit frightened of the ice storm story. No amount of soothing from either of them helped me overcome the nightmares. I was afraid it would come again, and being so little I'd die in it. I didn't want to die. I wanted to live, to run, and to play. Possibly one day, we'd all run up and down the field and explore all the wonderful things around us. Perhaps, if I teased them, I could get them to play. It would be their job to teach me about snow, the ways of the herd, and what my

place was. What did it mean to know your place? I
wondered.

If my mother's promise was to be kept, I had to
learn my place and become a part of their herd. Though
I still missed them both, each day it was harder to
remember her smell and the smell of Lucky.

My patience was wearing thin. Mother's words
seemed like a dream now—a dim memory. I needed to
look to my new family to teach me. But how could this
happen if I was shut away in this small enclosure or in
the barn? My aggravation was getting the better of me.
The need to run, play, and nuzzle my new friends grew.
When would the moment come that we could share our
lives? How could I find out what it took to be a big
horse if I wasn't to spend the days and nights with
them?

"When will they let me out?" I asked Chrome and
Connella.

They just looked at me. "They're the leaders of this
herd. They'll let you out when it's time. Be patient,
Dinky."

What was time? Why did I have to wait? After
spending a week between my stall and this little pen, my
dissatisfaction with my life was great. I fought Ken and

Marta when either of them tried to put me in the little paddock. It didn't matter that they were bigger and stronger than me. I was gaining weight and feeling bigger. My teeth were larger, and sooner or later I'd succeed. Then I saw how meekly Chrome and Connella followed them, and I wondered how could I win? Would my life be spent between this paddock and the stall?

"When can I become part of the family and herd?" I asked again and again. "Don't you understand it's not natural for horses to be alone? We're herd animals. Please, let me run free."

Seventeen

Freedom

> I fly through the sky
> On my hooves so spry
> Now I jump and play
> With my friends all day

Munching on my grain, I overheard Marta and Ken talking. "Ken, do you think it's time to let Dinky out in the field with Chrome and Connella?"

I was astonished. I held my breath waiting. Please, please, say yes. Finally he answered her, "Okay. We'll have to watch and see how it goes. We want to make sure he's safe."

I was to be free! I'd learn to be a part of the herd and share their lives. I'd run up and down the field as fast as I could go. I'd be able to learn my place.

Standing in awe, the sunlight poured on me, and Connella snapped, "Dinky, none of us will be going out in the field if you don't finish your breakfast."

"Sorry, Connella," I said and went back to eating. Not even her snapping at me could stop my happiness.

Chrome and Connella were out munching on their hay. I was done with my grain and waiting, praying, "Let it be true. Don't change your minds and put me in the little paddock. After glimpsing freedom, I wouldn't be able to take it again."

Sure enough, nearly as soon as my dish was empty, Ken came over, opened the door, and said softly, "Come on, Dinky. The day is here. Go run with your friends." He stood aside.

I looked at him, and then made a beeline for the field. I couldn't believe my luck, until Chrome put his ears back when I stood next to him to eat. "Move on, Dinky, this is my hay pile."

Quickly turning, I walked quietly over to Connella, only for her to look at me, ears back. What was wrong? Why wouldn't they let me eat with them? This never happened when I was with Lucky and Kaylee. Feeling dejected, I went over to a hay pile far away from my friends. Were they going to continue to treat me this way? I asked myself, would they ever let me eat and play with them? Feeling like an outsider again, I finally asked Connella. "Am I always going to be an outcast?"

"Dinky, you must learn the ways of the herd. One of the things you must learn is your place. You must understand who leads and who follows. Until you learn your place in the herd, it will go hard on you."

Throughout the day, I left them alone running up and down the field, my little brush of a tail high in the air. I practiced bucking just as I had seen them do. My muscles weren't coordinated enough, so I only achieved a little hop. Still, there were things I could play with alone and a world to explore. There was so much to see and do and so much to taste and feel. If it could get it into my mouth I nipped, chewed, or bit it, and then ran and jumped some more.

It was a beautiful day. I'd be happy and learn. If I wanted to be accepted into the herd, there was a lot I had to find out. Somehow I'd find a way to make them like me—I just had to. How could you make someone like you? What could I do? Was it like Connella said, I must learn to read the moods of the herd? It was hard to concentrate. There were so many new things to see and do—it all made me so excited.

Slowly I walked over to Chrome. "I'm smart. How am I to become skilled at something I've never been a part of if you don't explain?"

149

Sighing, Chrome turned to me with a long look and said, "Dinky, you must watch, you must listen, and you must hear the words of your elders. Then you will learn."

Even with my saddest and cutest face, he just turned away from me and went back to munching the hay. I wandered over to Connella and asked the same question. Turning to me, she put her ears back. She wouldn't talk to me right now. Was this what Chrome meant by watching and listening?

Finding a small patch of hay, I ate till my belly was full. Between bites, I made many trips to the water trough. Having my belly full was a new experience for me. I was too full of energy to stand around as Chrome and Connella were doing. There had to be something to get into.

Aha, there were Ken and Marta. What were they bringing into the field? Was the red thing that they were pushing a new toy? In their hands they had long sticks with bright colored things on the end of them. I wondered if they were going to teach me a new game. Happily I ran over to them and tasted first one stick then another.

Sadly, they wouldn't let me play with the sticks.
Perhaps I could push the red thing with the wheels. They
laughed as it fell over, dumping the manure into the
field. Regrettably, their laughter didn't last long and
they got exasperated with me. This new toy was just too
much fun. I couldn't stop myself. I had to play with
someone. Chrome and Connella glanced our way, and
soon they came over and chased me off. Ken and Marta
began talking sweetly to them and petting them. I felt
left out again wondering, where were my loves and
nuzzles? Why didn't they want me to be with them and
share Ken and Marta?

I tried to tell myself that this would pass. After all,
there had been many a time in the past when Lucky and
Kaylee ignored me. There were times when I would
walk away and ignore Kaylee. Those days were long
ago. It felt like a lifetime since I cuddled and played
with my friends. Oh, I knew that not even one moon
cycle had gone by. Remember, things would get better, I
thought.

Somehow I'd learn and become friends with my
new family. It was sad when Ken and Marta came to the
fence. After only a few minutes of them petting and
talking to me, either Chrome or Connella would soon be

there pushing me away to get all the attention. Alone and pouting, I hoped someday I'd be part of the fun. Would it always be this way? I thought feeling like the interloper again.

I knew my belly was always full, and there were many new things to do, though it seemed I'd never grow fast enough. I was still so much littler than all of them. I was much too small to play with them the way I played with Lucky and Kaylee. Sometimes I wondered why they adopted me. Did they honestly want me? Why was everyone so nice the first day? Now they didn't seem to want anything to do with me, and I felt like an outsider all the time.

"Stop it, Dinky," I told myself. "Keep in mind what Chrome and Connella told you: 'Dinky, you must learn the ways of the herd if you're to be part of it, and stop pouting. We'll play with you then. No one likes a whiner.' That's what they told me." So off I went to look in the woods by the back fence, and then lie down in the warm sun and take a nap dreaming of the day that I would run and play with them.

Hearing a noise in the driveway, my first thought was, "Please, don't let them give me away. I'm just beginning to learn."

Ken and a new man were at the fence. Ken was telling him my story. "Just maybe," I thought, "there might be some cuddles and attention for me." Joining them, I gave them kisses, and then happily turned, and running as fast as possible, I did a little leap in the air. The sound of their laughter filled the air. It was incredible.

But all too soon, over and again I was alone with my thoughts. Chrome and Connella were still hanging out together, and I knew I wasn't welcome yet. Maybe someday I would be. In the meantime, dusk was coming in, and soon it would be time for supper. The day was over. Possibly tomorrow I would fit in.

Eighteen

My Place

When I know all the rules,
I will learn to be good.
Somebody please help me
So I can learn now.

It was morning. The birds were singing in the trees. The geese were honking as they flew south. The days and nights were getting cooler. My little paddock was still standing there, almost like a monster ready to eat me should I refuse to learn.

I was waiting at the gate for Ken and Marta to come to feed us our breakfast. Out of nowhere came Chrome and Connella. Chrome gave me a nudge with his nose and a nip on the butt as he pushed between me and the gate. Connella moved behind him making a gesture with her head. I was to go behind her. This was a lesson in learning the order of things and my place in the herd. I didn't understand the need for this ritual. Lucky and I were equal, even though he was bigger and ate faster.

He never pushed me or chased me away. We shared. I liked sharing with my friends. It gave me a feeling of closeness and acceptance.

Perplexed again, I wondered why I couldn't share with Chrome and Connella. Why did Connella chase me off and Chrome push me away and nip me if I didn't go? What was this lesson that I was supposed to learn? Oh, I knew Connella told me that I needed to learn my place, but what exactly did that mean? What was my place? This was just too much for me. I'd never been part of a herd before. I wasn't even sure I knew how to be a horse yet.

Chrome went into his stall and Connella into hers. Ken and Marta closed their doors. "Dinky," Marta said, "go in your room. It's time for breakfast, little one."

Instead, I stood there looking first into Chrome's stall and next into Connella's with bewilderment all over my face. In my heart, I knew it was time for me to go into my room and have my breakfast. On the other hand, the need to share was still deep inside me. Now that I was out in the big field with Chrome and Connella, why was I still forced to eat alone without a friend to share with? Why couldn't we share a bucket or a pile of hay?

Marta put a rope on my halter and tried to sweet talk me into following her into my room. I planted my hooves and put my ears back. "Don't force me to eat alone again. Why can't they share with me the way Lucky used to do?"

Chrome and Connella were looking at me with impatience. We are all hungry. It felt like I always had to do things alone. Why couldn't I have stayed with Lucky? He liked me, he was my friend, and we always did everything together. We shared everything.

I was angry. Why did I have to live here where I didn't feel wanted? I stood my ground until I knew it wouldn't do me any good. Then reluctantly, I followed Marta into my room to have breakfast. I tried to nip her, annoyed and mad because I missed sharing with my friends from the big barn. I was weary of feeling like an exile and tired of having no one to play with. I ate my breakfast and waited to get let out with the big horses. "Please, let today be different from yesterday." I prayed that today I'd find out what my place meant and have someone to play with.

The sun was high in the sky. The birds were singing. Lying down to take my nap, I heard a car door slam and jumped to my feet. Someone had pulled up in the yard. Chrome and Connella came rushing over, herding me back to the far side of the field. They stood in front of me, blocking access to me. Chrome's head was low, his ears were back, and he was pawing the ground to show his aggression. Looking out I saw Carmen, the bad woman from the big barn. If this was to be my forever home, what was she doing here? "Please, don't let her take me back," I prayed. I didn't like her.

Marta came out of the house with her arms folded across her chest. She looked extremely angry. I wouldn't want to be in the bad woman's place for anything. Marta was looking at her with an icy glare in her eyes. I couldn't hear what they were saying, but Carmen seemed to be asking for something. Marta's expression got colder. Soon she pointed at the woman's car, and she went away. Before she got in her car and drove off, she turned to look at us. I was part of the herd, and I had a family. Chrome and Connella were protecting me, and Marta chased Carmen off. I thought, "I'm beginning to appreciate and recognize that they do love me."

After the bad woman had gone, Chrome and Connella moved off and began eating their hay again leaving me standing alone. My mind was racing with all that had happened. I had a warm feeling deep inside of me. I was a member of the herd, a part of a family that loved and protected me, and I wasn't alone.

Maybe, spending so much time thinking about what used to be made me imagine it better than it actually was. Had I missed seeing what I'd gained? I now knew a secret: they treasured me, and once I learned my place, just as Connella said, I would be happy.

I contemplated this and determined that tomorrow would be different. Beginning right then, I would watch and learn.

Nineteen

The Coyote

Dark is the night
Without moonlight.
Coyote prowls.
The horse does growl.

We wandered the meadow eating what was left of the hay leftover from last night's feeding. The nights were getting colder, and the stars were low in the sky, clearer and closer with the coming winter. Sometimes I lay in the fresh shavings in my room. I loved the smell and feel of fresh shavings and never could get enough of them, rolling in them until I was covered from nose to tail. Chrome and Connella took turns standing guard over me while I slept. Connella would stand next to me in my stall, and Chrome in front of the door protecting us both.

The sound of unearthly howling, crashing, and banging woke me and I jumped to my feet. Chrome was gone, and Connella was standing over me all puffed up.

Peeking over the wall, I saw a sight that made my heart race and my eyes go wide. I was terrified. There was a magnificent white horse in the front corner of our field rearing up on his hind legs, eyes glistening like fire, smoke pouring from his nose. Down he came with a thunderous crash. He was snorting, growling, and biting at the snarling creature that was cowering against the fence. Again and again he reared up kicking and biting at the creature. Connella made me stay behind her, but I had to see this warrior horse.

A light from the house came on. It was Ken coming to see what the ruckus was about. As he approached, the warrior horse backed off for an instant, and the creature escaped under the fence running for the woods across the road.

Ken spoke calmly to the great horse. My mind was racing from the sight of the battle. Who was the magnificent horse and where did he come from? Ken spoke to the illustrious warrior horse, "Good job, big guy. I don't think he'll be back again."

The warrior horse backed up slightly and snorted smoke from his nose. My mind raced. Where was Chrome? Did he sleep through the excitement? The warrior horse walked toward us, and I heard a familiar soft voice, "It's okay, Connella, you two can come out now."

Astonished, I realized the warrior horse was Chrome. He nuzzled Connella and me before walking off into the field as if nothing had happened. As he left, he turned to me and said, "We'll talk later."

I was bursting with excitement. I asked Connella what had just happened. "Was that creature a dog?"

"No," she said, yawning, "that was a coyote. They're a cowardly, sneaky lot, not to be trusted or tolerated at any time. It will be dawn soon. Calm down. Marta will be bringing out breakfast."

"But what about Chrome?" I asked.

"Leave him alone for now," she said as she watched Chrome walking away. She gave him the same look I had seen on my mother's face. Then she said, "Do you really think a mare would follow an alpha male who wasn't brave and courageous?" Then turning, she walked off into the predawn light.

I stood alone looking across the meadow. What had happened? How could my easy-going friend, Chrome, be such a warrior? How did he make smoke come from his nose? Would after breakfast be later? I felt very proud and protected by my new family and now knew they would make sure I was safe.

Before leaving, Ken stopped at the fence to reassure us that we were safe, and the sun would be up soon. Then he got into his large red truck and drove off leaving us alone in the chill of the early morning air. Shortly after he left, Marta came out and brought us our breakfast. It was the start of a new day. I was still excited by the events of last night and puzzled. How could they all act as if nothing happened? I wondered.

I wandered over to Chrome and stood next to him. Relaxed and eating our hay together, I asked, "Can we talk, Chrome?"

"Sure, kid, what's on your mind?"

"Will you please tell me about the coyote?"

Before he spoke, he looked deeply into my eyes. "They're about the largest predator around here, Dinky. Coyotes are sneaky, cowardly, and always on the prowl. They don't like horses, and we don't like them. They won't look you in the eye. Instead, they try to get behind you and bite the backs of your legs."

"Chrome, do you think Smitty, the dog at the old farm was a coyote?"

"No, Dinky, humans never tame coyotes. You need to remember the smell of the coyote. Someday it might be your job to protect the herd. Not for a long time, but someday." Then he started to walk away.

I asked, "Chrome, how did you make smoke come out of your nose?"

Looking back smiling, he said, "You'll learn, kid. You'll learn," and continued to walk away.

*T*wenty

Uncle Kris

Teasing friends is my delight
So long as there is no fright.
Surgery or games today,
No time to waste on dismay.

I was growing rapidly, gaining height and weight, playing tag, running in the field, chomping on hay, watching the birds, deer, and other animals. The changes in my body felt good. Soon I would be grown. Marta and Ken were over by the fence laughing at me again.

"Look at Dinky," Marta pointed. "He truly is Chrome's little shadow. See how he follows him."

"You should see them, when you're at work, honey. They eat together, and he teases Chrome unmercifully. It's especially true when they're all wearing their halters. He really gets Chrome's goat then, pulling on it without sympathy until he plays. It usually ends up with the three of them playing tag. He's lucky Chrome is a patient, good sort of horse with a laid back way about him," Ken replied.

"What does he do to get one of them to play if they aren't in their halters?"

"Funny you should ask. He follows Chrome around the meadow pulling on his tail. It's hysterical. He doesn't find it as easy with Connella. You know how she is. If she's not in the mood, she'll put her ears back and give him, her not now look. He usually leaves her alone then. He's learning when to move on."

I looked around, bored with just listening to them talk. Chrome was napping, and Connella didn't look in an exceptionally pleasant frame of mind. Maybe I'd go play with the orange cones, or the round purple things, but it would be more fun to play tag. It was my favorite game even if I was the smallest and last to the finish line. Oh well, it didn't look like either of them were in the mood right then. I wished Ken and Marta would come in the meadow and play, but they didn't seem interested either. They were just sitting at the table talking. So I kicked one of the round purple balls around. Oh well, it would be supper time soon. "I saw Sir Owl last night while you were napping, Chrome. He's really beautiful. I like the 'who who' sound he makes. I'm curious. Do you know why Ken and Marta put halters on you and Connella today? I know I usually have mine on, but you two usually don't."

"Dinky, I think Uncle Kris is coming today. He's nice, but not a lot of fun. We get poked and prodded a lot," Chrome said sounding a bit bothered.

Who was Uncle Kris? I wondered what terrible things he would do to me. If Chrome, who was so powerful, felt helpless when it came to Uncle Kris, how was I to protect myself? He didn't seem afraid of Uncle Kris. It was just that he knew he was the boss, and we had to mind him.

The day was sunny, crisp, and clear, and the leaves on the trees were turning all sorts of bright colors. They looked so gorgeous. If only the flies would leave us alone.

"I hate the flies, Chrome."

"Don't worry. The flies will go away soon. If not today, then tomorrow. They can't live when it gets colder."

"I hope so. I'm tired of them buzzing around and biting."

Our hay, still only half eaten, was sitting in the field. Uncle Kris was there, and we were all shut up in our rooms. I liked him. His voice was unusually gentle. "He's growing nicely," He told Marta and Ken as he put his hands on me, checking me out everywhere. "He's ready for his operation. We can do it next month when the flies are gone, or we can wait till spring."

I didn't like the sound of that at all. What was an operation? It sounded terrible.

"No, it's important that his operation is as soon as possible. We don't want to linger until next spring. If the weather warms up too early and the flies come back, it'll have to wait. It would be terrible if he matured early and we had a stallion on our hands. That would cause no end of problems now and in the future for them all."

"It's possible that we could have an early spring. Okay, we'll plan on a month from now."

What would Uncle Kris do to me next month? Why didn't he stop touching me? I felt trapped in my room with Marta holding me.

Uncle Kris's hands were gentle as he petted me. "Which shots has he had?" he asked Marta.

She listed all the shots I'd been given at the big stable.

"Good. Then I'll see him in a month," he said as he left my room.

Following them out, I was curious about what would happen to my friends. I pushed my nose through the window into their room. Ken pulled me away from them so I couldn't get a really close look. Chrome stood patiently while he got his shots. When Uncle Kris put his hand into Chrome's mouth, Chrome put up a quite a fuss and jumped around a bit.

Finally, Connella's turn came. She stood quietly while the needles were poked into her, and Uncle Kris fooled around with his hand in her mouth. She didn't seem to mind the attention at all.

"They'll all need their teeth done in the spring," I heard Uncle Kris say. What did that mean? When he said "all," did that mean me too? I hoped to escape having his hands in my mouth again.

Patting all of us, he left. Marta let us out of our rooms to finish our breakfast, and the three of them went over to Uncle Kris's truck and stood talking with him.

Looking over at them and worrying, I asked, "Chrome, what's an operation?"

"Depends on what needs doing. I needed stitches under my chin once right after we first moved here. Connella and I had been playing, and she kicked me quite hard. But I think they called that surgery, not an operation. When I was little like you, I had the operation; it's nothing to worry about. Most young males get the operation. For a few days, you're a little uncomfortable, but it's not a big deal. You always worry too much, Dinky."

Twenty-one

Growing Up

Finally getting settled
A new life now begun
Operation to come
Only for boys not girls

Frost had been on the ground the last few nights, and that morning I noticed the flies were gone. Just like Chrome said, the flies didn't like the cold weather. Chrome and Connella were in a fine mood playing like foals. They liked the cooler weather. All too soon they wandered off for some private time, and both of them put their ears back when I wandered over to see if they'd play again.

I was learning the signs and language of the herd, knowing when not to bother them. Feeling alone again, standing there looking at my friends, I thought about my lost friends, Lucky and Kaylee. I hoped they were happy and wondered what they were doing. Had they gone to live with their families, or were they still living at the big stable? I wondered.

A few lonely leaves were still hanging on the tree branches. All the rest of the leaves were swirling around on the ground, bright rainbows of light. I loved to watch them, and sometimes we even ate a few.

Uncle Kris just drove up in his white truck. Oh no, was this the day of my operation? Standing and trembling in Connella's room, I watched Marta and Ken at Uncle Kris's truck. The time seemed all too short, and yet it felt like forever before they walked over and all came into the room with me. Even though they were talking sweetly to me and petting me, I felt cornered, terrified to have all three of them in there with me. It made me agitated, especially when Uncle Kris poked me with a needle. Then I really jumped around. I was too groggy and sleepy after that, though still able to hear their voices and feel Uncle Kris's hands touching me. Their words didn't make sense. "The operation is finished," Uncle Kris said.

They all stayed in the room with me for a while, talking and petting me. I was having a hard time balancing myself. My legs were extremely wobbly. At last I was out in the meadow again, though I didn't feel like myself at all yet. Not ready to see anyone, I hid behind the barn. Then, just as Chrome told me it would be, I found myself a bit uncomfortable and sore, but not in pain. Connella didn't understand all the fuss. After sniffing me, she just turned and walked away.

"Connella seems a bit put out, Chrome."

"She likes her attention, Dinky. Though I don't think she would want an operation. Still she feels left out. Besides she's a mare, and mares don't have these kinds of operations."

The day was nearly gone. I was running a bit, though a little slower, and I wasn't jumping yet. Perhaps Chrome was right and in few days I'd have forgotten the operation.

Twenty-two

Visitors

> Small is the cow bird
> Who follows the herd
> Ready to receive
> And eat what we leave.

If there were no visitors or lessons that day, I'd run up and down the field and make the leaves fly around the ground. I was so happy. My belly was full, and there was enough attention for all of us. I loved the brushing and petting. I was glad the crawly feeling I used to have in my belly at the old stable was gone.

The day before Ken and Marta had taken us all for a walk after breakfast. We had to stop, walk, and back up when we were told. Chrome was much better at this, but I was learning. It was funny to watch Connella. She was very good when she wanted to be, but she could be terribly stubborn.

There was my new friend over by the fence waiting for me. She was a very amicable woman with yellow hair, a soft voice, and terribly sad eyes. I trotted over, eagerly looking forward to my pets, treats, and whatever story she'd tell me that day. I'd make her eyes shine again, and for a little while they wouldn't be sad, I thought.

"When I was young, little one, I had horses that lived with me, and I miss them very much," she said while petting me. Her need for a friend was strong that day, so even when the little carrots were gone I stayed a while. I gave her one more kiss before I ran into the wide meadow. Its call was too much to wait any longer. Later I'd take my nap in the warm sun when it beckoned me to sleep.

A bright red truck pulling into the driveway woke me from my nap. A very large man with a soft, gentle voice was talking to Ken at the fence. I'll go meet them, I thought, trotting over. The big man held out his hand for me to sniff. It was very strong when he patted me. I wanted him to see how powerful I was too. I turned and ran all the way around the field before going back to the fence. The two of them stood there laughing at me. When I got back to them, they both petted me again. It was fun when we had visitors.

The afternoon sun was fearfully hot. We were all lazy, just standing around grazing. Usually the heat didn't bother me as much as it did my friends, but today for some reason, it was making me sleepy. Before napping, I had to know. I was still so curious. Connella wasn't asleep so I'd ask her, "What kind of birds are the little brown ones that come to visit us in the field? It seems that they're always under my feet."

"Dinky, they're called cow birds."

I looked at her mystified. "Connella, there were cows at the farm where I use to live before I went to the big stable. They were very big and brown. I didn't see any of them with wings or flying."

Looking at me with a twinkle in her kind, brown eyes, she said, "I think they're named cow birds because they're brown and follow cows and horses around to eat the little bits we leave behind."

This made sense to me. The little birds were fun. Now I'd laugh when I saw them and think about cows with wings.

"Dinky, when they're around we're safe, for they fly away when trouble is near," she finished.

Ms. Fisher Cat was running by the meadow again. Her long, slim, brown body was exceedingly strange-looking. She seemed to be very busy today, barely nodding at me when I said hi. Usually she gave me a quick hello before she was off into the woods or across the street.

Waking from my nap, I heard noises coming from the woods behind the meadow. I ran as fast as possible to the fence, but still I missed them. All that was left was the sound of dainty footsteps running back into the woods.

Turning to Chrome I asked, "What made that noise?"

"They're called deer, and they're timid. If you want to meet them, you must stand quite still when they come around."

I decided the next time I heard them, I would do this. Luckily, I didn't have long to wait. Looking up, I saw them near the fence again. They were very unusual looking creatures, a little smaller than me with brown fur, enormous dark eyes, and long, shiny legs. One of them had pointy sticks on his head. Excited, I rushed to the fence. Unfortunately, it was just as Chrome said. In a flash, they were gone with only their white tails showing as they ran back into the woods. How beautiful, fast, and small they were, I thought, standing there in awe.

Still thinking about the beautiful deer and all the other creatures that I had seen since coming there, I noticed Peeping Tom Turkey walking by. I had seen him on other occasions when he came down from the woods in the back, but I'd never been so close to him before. He was a very strange-looking big bird. His head was red with no feathers, and he had long skinny legs and a large round body with gray feathers. When he walked it was with a long stride, his head wobbling back and forth. He seemed a grumpy sort, but I remembered Ole Jack and decided to make conversation.

"Hello, Peeping Tom," I said. I called him that because I'd heard Marta tell Ken about him, and that's what she called him.

He looked at me, stretched up as tall as he could get, and then began flapping his wings at me and making a gobbling sound.

"Why are you all alone?" I asked, ignoring his flapping about.

He looked at me standing there unafraid. "I am alone because I choose to be. I like adventure and most of my family doesn't."

"Why do you peek in the windows of the house?" I asked, feeling braver.

"I already told you, I'm curious about the world," he said as he ran off, looking remarkably clumsy on his two legs, wings held tightly at his side.

Standing there after he left, looking around me and thinking about all my new friends, I realized how much fun it was when they came to visit. My family loved and cared for me, and I was no longer alone. I hoped tomorrow I would be as happy as I was today.

Twenty-three

Games

> Happy now is the little foal
> Cleaning out the water trough
> Not a chore just a game

Ken and Marta had such marvelous toys to play with and were always doing such fascinating things around the farm. It was hard to decide which one was my favorite. For instance, they had a noisy, green and yellow thing that they climbed onto and rode around the yard. Connella said it was called a tractor. We all got intensely excited when one of them rode it around the fence blowing fresh cut grass into our field. We followed it, only stopping long enough to eat the sweet grass it threw into the meadow.

Earlier when Ken was finished throwing grass into the meadow, he drove it along the fence. I raced it and almost won! Chrome and Connella laughed at me, but I knew soon I would be faster than that tractor.

179

Then we were working on the barn. They lifted large pieces of wood, and Marta held them while Ken used a blue thing connected to a bright orange hose. At first I tried to help Marta hold the wood, but Ken's toy looked like more fun. It made very loud pops, and then the wood stayed on the side of the barn.

Connella didn't mind the noise, but Chrome hated it. He stood at the far end of the field looking lonely and pouting. Connella joined him so he wouldn't be by himself. Maybe in a little while, I'd go down to visit him for a bit. I did feel badly for Chrome, except it was just too much fun to stay away for long. It didn't matter that it was noisy and smelly; I just had to get my nose up close to check it out.

Laughing at me, Ken said, "Marta, I think Dinky will grow up to be a carpenter."

I wasn't sure what that was, but it sounded like fun. Especially if it meant I could play with their toys, like the ones that make a loud pop or blew grass into the meadow. Making people laugh was my favorite thing. This afternoon Uncle Kevin came over to help Ken put the wood on the roof of our run-in shelter. He laughed extremely loud when I pulled on his blue pants.

There were many jobs that helped entertain me, but I believed my most important job was making people laugh. There was one job that I considered to be my regular job. That morning I was fortunate. I saw Ken come out of the little shed with the long handled brush. That meant we would be cleaning the water trough. I liked to put my nose in the water and splash around while he was using the brush. Chrome and Connella decided to help too. It made Marta laugh so hard standing there watching the three of us crowded into the trough with Ken and the brush.

Boy oh boy, it was going to be a fun day. We were going to play at cleaning out the stalls and cleaning the field. These were more of my other favorite chores. Even though it was such fun to play with the long handled stick, it was even more fun to dump the red rolling thing over. Unfortunately, I think they figured me out, because they locked me in my room to make sure I couldn't help. I'd asked Chrome and Connella why they didn't let me learn to push it too. They just looked at me and said, "Kids," and walked away.

The next morning Ken brought the green tractor into the meadow. It had a black trailer connected to the back of it. Connella said it was hers and wouldn't let me play with it. She was very possessive about it. She stood right next to it. I could only get close to the black thing on the back. Ken and Marta were loading it with sticks that were on the ground. Connella didn't care about the black thing on the back, so I helped them load it. Chrome was more interested in getting his pets. He wasn't interested in the tractor.

It was lots of fun learning about all these things, and it kept me extremely busy. Ken was right; I just might be a carpenter when I grew up or maybe a farmer. Then I could drive the green tractor around. That would undoubtedly tweak Connella. What a wonderful idea that was. She got so serious about everything sometimes.

Twenty-four

Snow!!!

> Winter wonderland,
> White and oh so grand.
> Cold fun for the foal.
> Dinky learns to roll.

Dawn broke clear and bright, and the geese were honking as they flew south for the winter. The three of us were still eating the pickings left over from the night before. Marta had just come out to give us our breakfast.

Chrome was always first into his stall, and then Connella. Looking at the both of them, I waited as I did every morning. Soon Marta would put the rope on my halter and lead me into my room for breakfast. Connella started teasing Chrome, getting him all riled up, and Chrome began jumping around and kicking the stall. Marta scolded them both. Stopping, they looked at her, yawned, and stood quietly while she went to get our grain. I was pleased. Chrome didn't feel the necessity to kick the stall a few more times that morning. If he had,

Marta would have scolded him again from the little building that held our food with a, "Chrome, stop it." It would have delayed breakfast, and I was hungry.

Just as we finished our grain and the hay was lying in the meadow, the snow began. It was clean, white, and cold as it landed on my back. It was so pretty. I stuck out my tongue, tasting the white flakes that were falling. The snowflakes made the sky gray and cloudy. There would probably not be a nap in the sun that day. Chrome and Connella were flying up and down the field in their excitement, jumping high in the air, and although I ran as fast as my little legs could carry me, I couldn't keep up with them.

"Wait for me," I yelled.

Putting their ears back, and looking at me, they said, "You're too little to play these games with us, Dinky."

It snowed all morning. Soon the whole meadow was covered in the white powder. Chrome and Connella were rolling in it and running around the field. With my brush of a tail straight up, I ran with them. We all stopped now and then to take a bite of hay until it was covered in white. Then Chrome and Connella pawed the ground, stuck their noses into the snow, pulled and uncovered the hay underneath. I tried to follow suit.

Unfortunately, my hooves were smaller, so I followed them eating what they uncovered.

The three of us were having a grand time, rolling, running, jumping, and kicking the snow high in the air. It tasted like nothing I'd ever tasted before. It was so cold with a flavor of frozen rain that tickled my tongue.

"Dinky, the first snow is the best to eat," Connella said.

Regrettably, the sun came out warming up the day. The sun was so bright it hurt my eyes, so I kept them half closed. Even though I loved the snow, it was time for my morning nap. Finding a good place in the sun on top of a pile of hay by the water tub, I laid down to sleep. Just before I fell asleep, I heard Chrome say, "Soon it'll all melt, the day will be too warm, and the meadow will get muddy, so we must enjoy it while it's here. In a few weeks or a month it will fall and stay on the ground."

Waking up from my nap, I saw that most of the snow was brown. Connella came over to me and said, "Dinky, don't eat the brown snow. Only eat the white snow."

I looked at her and wondered why she thought she had to tell me this. Of course, I wouldn't eat the brown snow. It was full of mud. I wasn't stupid, but knowing she meant it kindly, I only said, "Thank you."

The leaves were all gone from the trees. When we looked over the back fence, it was a strange, new world. The branches of the trees were heavy with snow, and off in the distance I saw lumps of things. I asked, but not even Chrome or Connella knew what they were. "It's like that every year," Connella told me. "We keep an eye on them. Maybe someday we'll find out what they are."

The little monster of a paddock was still sitting in the meadow. Oh, how I wished it was gone. I worried every day that Ken and Marta would put me back in it and I'd lose this glorious, vast field to run in. If that happened, I was concerned my growing relationship with Chrome and Connella would be gone, and once again I'd lose my place.

It did have its uses though. When Connella or Chrome scolded me or I felt the need to get away from them, I'd go into the little paddock. I much preferred going behind the barn where they couldn't reach me because they were too bulky. Then I'd sneak out and nip one of them. That usually worked to get them to play and chase me all over the meadow. And we played hide and seek. I truly wished the little paddock was gone.

Huge, fluffy, white flakes were falling out of the sky again. Glorious, wonderful snow! Chrome and Connella were right. It had come back. I could hardly wait until the field was covered in it again. I could stand for hours just letting it fall on my back and head. Then I'd run up and down the meadow, roll and jump and play. Except when a particularly noisy truck came by, there was a hush over everything. "What's that noise?"

"It's the snow plow coming, Dinky. Watch how it pushes the snow high into the air clearing the road."

Soon all we could see were small splotches of white on the black road. Just as Chrome had said she would, Connella put her nose down into the high snow on one end of the field and was running, throwing her head back and forth. She was playing snow plow. The snow scattered high in the air, and we had a road down our field too.

It looked like so much fun, I had to try. Both of them laughed their heads off at me as I stood with a snoot full of snow hanging from my nose.

We watched Ken until the banks along the edge of the driveway got so tall we couldn't see him. We could still hear the noise and see the snow blow high in the air but could no longer see the red machine he was pushing. I was content to be alive in this cold, white paradise. All the trees were barren of leaves and covered in white. Everything was new and different. Even the cars made less noise as they drove by in this winter wonderland.

The cars on the street kept stopping to watch Chrome roll over on his back and kick the snow up in the air. Marta said we were making snow angels. We ran, jumped, rolled and played. Even Chrome and Connella acted like they were foals again.

The more I understood the ways of our herd, the less time I spent in Coventry. I didn't like being in Coventry. It was hard to be ignored after being scolded and told to think about it. Sometimes I didn't understand what I was supposed to think about. It was just like Chrome told me, the more I learned the ways of the herd, the happier we all would be. Now I ate next to them in the meadow. Mostly they didn't mind me trying to get them to play even when they weren't in the mood. Ken and Marta spent a lot of time with us, and I was learning what a treat was. My treats were broken into little pieces. My mouth was still too small for the big treats. The world was marvelous, the days and nights were cold, and the stars were so low in the sky. After eating our hay at night, we went into our rooms to dry off from a day spent playing in the snow. Sometimes, we napped in our warm rooms or wandered the field.

Our winter fur was thick now and puffed up keeping us warm. I was glad I didn't have to wear a long thing on me like Connella told me some horses did. I remembered what she said, "Dinky, sometimes in the winter at the other barn, Chrome and I would see a horse from the herd standing covered nearly to its feet in some brightly colored cloth. It wasn't like a saddle or the pad that was put on our backs before we took Marta and Ken out for a ride. It was longer and covered them so far down that they couldn't comfortably run or roll. We would hear them complain about it, especially when it got wet. And then they'd be colder than we were even when we had icicles hanging off us. Their winter coats wouldn't grow thick, and they had trouble keeping up with us running and playing. We would hear the humans say it was to protect them from the cold because they were older or a bit under the weather. I know I don't want to have a blanket on me," she added.

Thinking long and hard, I decided I didn't want a blanket either. It didn't sound like fun, except maybe to chew on. The days were much shorter. Ken and Marta stopped feeding me grain three times a day. There was enough hay in the meadow; I wasn't as interested in the grain. I didn't like getting locked in my room and having to leave my friends while I ate. We only ate our grain in separate rooms in the morning and at night. Once we were finished with our grain, we'd graze on the hay that they put out in the field for us. Wandering the big meadow, we ate a little here and a little there as horses do. Now that it was winter, Ken and Marta didn't sit outside with us at night as often. When Marta got home from work it was dark, and she stopped by the fence and turned on our light, so she could give us a cookie and a cuddle before saying goodnight.

One morning we watched Ken and Marta put up colored lights around the house. Across the street we could see others doing the same thing. The lights were beautiful and glimmered at night, twinkling like the stars in the sky except they weren't white. They were very colorful and pretty. Every day there was something new happening that we could watch and find intriguing. If it wasn't human visitors, it was the deer, Peeping Tom Turkey, or Ms. Fisher Cat.

Earlier that morning, we'd seen a coyote across the
street in the woods. Chrome herded Connella and me
into the back of the field. Then he stood guard making
sure the coyote wouldn't come over to harm us. I didn't
much like it when I had to stay put, but one look at
Chrome all puffed up, ears back, eyes looking over the
fence into the wood, and I knew I must mind him. Boy, I
really wouldn't like to be on his bad side like that coyote
was. I was fortunate with a family to protect me. The
most Chrome or Connella did to me when they were
annoyed was to give me a small nip. If I didn't listen,
they'd put their ears back and give me their not now,
I'm not in the mood look.

There was excitement in the air. Chrome and
Connella said, "Its Christmas, Dinky."

Wondering what Christmas was, I asked Chrome.

I listened with rapture as Chrome explained to me,
"Dinky, you've been watching the bright lights across
the street and on Marta and Ken's house for a few weeks
now, right?"

"Yes," I answered, breathlessly waiting for his
response.

"Well, they're for Christmas, and today is
Christmas morning. On Christmas morning we get

special treats with our breakfast. We each get an entire basket full of apples, carrots and cookies."

Chrome went on, "Connella's quite funny. If Ken and Marta don't take the dishes away from us, she'll carry her dish all over the field wanting more treats. It's a wonderful day, Dinky. You'll love your presents too. Each Christmas we each get something unique along with our Christmas baskets. One year I got a new saddle that was lighter on my back, and Connella got a handsome bridle and new halter. I wonder what we'll get this year."

It felt like hours waiting for the special treats to come. All of us stood at the fence in anticipation. We could see that the lights were on in the house, so we knew they were up. All wide eyed and excited, I couldn't leave my place at the fence—not even when Chrome and Connella wandered off. I'd never had Christmas and could hardly wait till Ken and Marta brought out our baskets full of treats.

I'd never had apples before and wasn't sure if I'd like them, so I left them in the dish. Later I saw Connella go into my room. I noticed after she came out that the apples were gone. Maybe next time I'd try them.

I'm not sure if I will like the new blanket that tied around my stomach. I'd so much rather have had a new ball or even a leather halter like Chrome and Connella got, but Connella said my head was too small for a leather halter and I would have to wait till I was bigger.

Twenty-five

Uncle Bob

> Now Dinky has a home
> From which he won't roam.
> He never thinks to leave,
> He only thinks to cleave.

The days were getting longer. It was now light out when Marta came home from work. She stopped at the fence for a visit before going into the house. The snow had melted from the meadow, and the ground was no longer hard. Our wonderful meadow was one big mud pit because of the rain and the melting snow. It wasn't fun to run and play when we had to watch every step. We were all muddy from rolling to keep the bugs off of us. I didn't remember ever seeing so many kinds of bugs. There were flying ones and crawling ones. Some of them would bite and leave substantial welts on Chrome, which made him very unhappy. We were all quite crabby with the nuisance of the bugs, the mud, and the constant rain.

"Chrome, I'm not sure I like spring."

"Don't worry, Dinky, soon the rains will stop, and the ground will dry. Then Marta will put some stuff on us to keep the bugs away," Chrome answered, tail swishing.

Chrome and Connella continued to promise me that soon the days would be sunny and dry, but I couldn't remember ever going through this type of weather. I was nearly a year old now, and my past seemed a distant memory. Sometimes I still thought of Lucky, but it was becoming harder to remember his face and smell. Even my dreams of Mother were hazier now. Soon I'd be a colt and no longer a foal.

It was fun to meet new people, but Chrome only let me meet new people if Ken or Marta was around. Each time I heard one of them ask Ken, "How much for the little black one?" I still held my breath waiting. I didn't want to leave my family. I wanted to live with them forever. "Please, let me stay. Please want me and let me stay," I'd say over and over to myself.

Then Ken would tell whoever it was, "You don't have enough money to buy him," or "How much would you sell your kid for?"

Then I was sure they wanted me. It made me feel safe and happy. Before I ran off to play with my friends, I stopped, nuzzled, and gave Ken kisses. Though I still worried a little sometimes.

A white truck pulled up in the driveway. Ken and Marta came out of the house. It was Uncle Bob. I remembered him from the old stable. He had picked up my feet and messed with them. I remember how nice he smelled, but I also remembered how his messing with my feet brought back awful memories—memories of the barn on parade day.

"Chrome, do you like getting your feet messed with?" I asked as we all stood at the fence watching Uncle Bob unload his things.

"It's quite nice, Dinky. I don't kick myself in the back of my legs when my hooves are trimmed. Connella likes the feeling of being pampered."

I thought about this as Marta put me on the cross ties. Chrome and Connella were in their rooms waiting for their turns. "How are you, little guy?" Uncle Bob said as he petted me.

I stood very quietly as he picked my feet up, cleaned my hooves and trimmed them. After he finished, he turned to Marta. "He has come a long way, hasn't he?

Quite the little gentleman now," Uncle Bob said petting me. I walked proudly into my room to wait for Chrome and Connella to get their feet done, and I realized a unpleasant memory had been replaced by a good one today.

Twenty-six

Birthdays

Now a yearling he has become,
Already tall and more to come.
Never to roam, always a home,
Happy now no longer alone.

The morning bloomed brightly. The sun was shining, and the birds were coming back from wherever they spent the winter. Probably in the south like my mother told me, I thought. Marta stopped at the fence to give us cookies and cuddle me. It was my birthday. The night before, Ken and Marta had talked about the party they were going to have for us in a few days on Chrome's birthday. At first I was a little put out that the party wouldn't be on my birthday. Then Chrome told me Marta didn't have to go to work on his birthday. That was why they were waiting, so the whole family would be there to celebrate our birthdays. It wouldn't be the same to have a party without Marta.

"Chrome," I asked, "do you think our birthday party will be like Christmas?"

"Maybe a little, Dinky, but it's not the same. That's why Connella is a bit put out it isn't her party too. She knows she'll get the same treats as we do, but she'd like it to be her day too."

I woke to the noise of Sir Owl saying, "Goodnight, I'm going to sleep now." I was excited, because it was the day of our party. It would be a tremendously fun day. I just knew it.

I was a yearling now and happy. It was funny to hear them sing, "Happy Birthday to you," as they gave us our breakfast singing both of our names.

Marta said. "You are growing so big and strong, Dinky. What a beautiful boy you are."

She reminded me of my mother's words to me. For a moment, it was if I could smell her again. I proudly strutted around the field looking for mischief to get into. After all, I was growing up. My memories of the dark, scary times were dimmer, buried by the love of my family.

Once in a while I still went off by myself when the memories came back. I didn't like to think of the dark times, but when the memories returned I felt afraid and alone again. Luckily, this only happened when I was reprimanded by one of my family. Then I remembered the days when my future seemed so bleak and Lucky and I would tell each other stories to try to cheer ourselves up. I always remembered the words of my mom before they took me from her, "Dinky, you are beautiful and will grow up to be a lovable horse. Don't forget to keep your sweetness, and when you find your home, listen to your herd and learn their ways. If you do, you will be happy and safe."

That day I was determined not to go into that dark place. It was my birthday and I would have fun. A yearling now, I was no longer a small foal whose fate was in jeopardy each day. My belly was always full. I had friends, a family, plenty of room to run and play, and there was always something to investigate. If I was bored, I could take the bars out from between Chrome and Connella's rooms and play with them. Then I'd laugh when Marta and Ken came out and found them all over the place. They'd get an extremely confused look on their faces. Chrome and Connella would hang their heads and look guilty. It was so funny because they felt guilty, but it was me and I didn't feel guilty. It was fun.

Now it was spring and soon it would be summer. Ken had just come out of the little shed with the long handled brush. I knew just what he was going to do. He was going to play the clean our water trough game, my favorite. It always amused me, and I loved to help him. However, it was my birthday and I was feeling a bit mischievous, not really in the mood for the usual routine. I wanted something a bit different today and hoped to get my wish. Chrome loved to drink from the clean tub as it filled with the fresh, clear water. Out of the corner of my eye, I saw him waiting for Ken to stop cleaning and start filling.

Then I got lucky. Ken walked away to turn on the hose that filled the tub but left the yellow brush on the fence. I grabbed it before he came back. I chased Chrome up and down the meadow with my new toy. When Ken got back, we played a new game. "Oh ho, you want to play tug of war," I heard him say as we fought over the yellow brush. At last, he got the brush away from me and went back to the hose. He put the hose into the trough and walked away again, this time with brush in hand.

I thought he went to put the brush away, but I wasn't sure. I was too busy watching the green hose wiggle all around as the water came through it filling the trough. Chrome joined me and was drinking the fresh, cold water. Not able to stand it any longer, I picked up the hose with my mouth and accidentally sprayed Chrome in the face. Oh, how he jumped in the air before he ran off! Aha, I thought, Chrome doesn't like to get his face wet. Off I ran, hose in my mouth chasing him, determined to catch and spray him again. I seldom got the better of Chrome, and it was downright fun. Out of the corner of my eye, I saw Ken coming back out of the shed.

He took one look at the situation, climbed over the fence, and we began another game of tug of war. By the time the game ended we were both wet all over, and Ken was laughing. So I knew that even if I hadn't made Chrome happy, I'd made Ken happy. Ken finally won that game too. I was afraid he'd never again leave the hose unmanned. Surely he'd stand guard over it if I was near. I knew he'd still hold it for me to get a drink. Chrome loved to drink from the trough as it was filling, and I enjoyed drinking from the hose. So we were both happy, though I did hope Ken would leave the hose unattended again so I could chase Chrome with it.

Our party lasted almost the whole day. Connella got the same amount of treats, nuzzling, brushing, and playing as we did. Marta and Ken spent most of the day with us—even at nap time. They sat at their table and watched over us as we rolled in the dirt, played, and napped in the field. Such a wonderful day, and I didn't mind that Chrome and I shared our birthdays. We all felt loved and celebrated.

Twenty-seven

Belonging

> My name is Dinky. I'm smart.
> I'm growing up a sweetheart.
> Big and tall I will become,
> Strong and sure it will be done.

The birds were singing loudly, the insects were humming, and there was a fresh breeze in the air. It was late spring, the rains had stopped, and the sun was bright. Before breakfast, each of us had to get into our halters. We were all smart, so we knew this meant we were going to have a new experience that day. Maybe we'd get to go run in the round pen after breakfast or be brushed. Just maybe it would be something we wouldn't like very much.

I really hoped it would be a chance to run in the round pen, even though I really didn't understand yet what was expected of me. It was so much fun to run around as fast as I could go stretching and feeling the muscles in my body become stronger. Even so I was a bit worried. Chrome told me he'd heard them talk about Uncle Kris coming back. I still remembered the last time he came when I had my operation, and I didn't like the idea at all. Even though I liked Uncle Kris a lot, he always seemed to do something decidedly unpleasant to one of us.

Chrome was right again. Not long after breakfast, Uncle Kris' white truck pulled up in the yard, and we were all back in our rooms. Uncle Kris felt me all over. "He's going to be at least Chrome's size, maybe up to seventeen hands. By the time he's about eight years old he'll be nearly white like Chrome is," he told Marta and Ken.

So astounded, I stopped jumping around and trying to get away from the poking and prodding. In such awe, I almost forgot to try and bite him when he put the needles in me to give me my spring shots.

Recalling again what my mother had said, "Dinky, you will probably end up being white like me and grow up to be a large, strong horse." But to be bigger than Chrome! I knew that would never be. I'd always be Chrome's little brother. Chrome would always be bigger than me. He was alpha male, and I would always be smaller, but I was happy that I'd be white like him and my mother. I was glad I'd have the life my mother promised me. I knew I would always remember her words that fateful day, "Remember, I will always watch over you."

Uncle Kris was finished with me. I stood outside Chrome and Connella's stalls and watched Uncle Kris give them their shots and put metal things into their mouths. The sound was horrible as he scraped away at their teeth. Chrome was nearly asleep from the shots, and even though his head was nearly on the floor, I could tell he hated the whole thing.

Uncle Kris said, "Dinky has a wolf's tooth coming in. It will have to be taken out in the fall. Let's hope the other one comes in by then so I can do both at once."

What did this mean, a wolf's tooth? I didn't like the sound of that or when he said they'd have to be taken out. I knew I'd ask Chrome and Connella about it later when they were more awake and didn't have those metal things hanging out of their mouths.

Uncle Kris left. We were all once again out in the meadow eating hay. I noticed the birds were still singing and the hawks flying overhead. The sky was still blue and the breeze was blowing. "Uncle Kris, said I had a wolf's tooth. Chrome, what's a wolf's tooth? Is it like a coyote?"

Chrome looked sleepily at me with his big brown eyes, yawned, and said, "Dinky, you are not a coyote."

At times Connella was the deeper thinker, so I asked her, "Connella, what's a wolf's tooth? Is it like a coyote?"

She laughed at me, turned, and sauntered away still chuckling, not even bothering to answer me.

I didn't think they knew what a wolf's tooth was either, but at least I didn't think it was like a coyote anymore. Tired from the trials of the day, I decided to lie down and take a nap. It was hot and I felt lazy. I picked a spot in the sun close to the water trough and in head's reach of a hay pile. That way when I woke, I could just lie there and have a snack without getting up. Falling asleep, I dreamed of my mother and again heard her words, "Dinky, you are smart. You are beautiful. You will grow big and strong. Someday you might be white like me when you grow up."

In my dream I told her all about my new life. I told her of the trials and sorrows, the hunger and fear of the first months, and how much I had missed her and hoped to one day see her again. I told her of Lucky and that without him I might not have made it. And I told her of Chrome, Connella, Ken, Marta, and our home.

We talked about my birthday party, the fun I had, and what Uncle Kris had said to Marta and Ken earlier. I told her I was learning the ways of my herd and had a forever family who loved me and nuzzled me when I needed it. We talked about the different bugs, the snow, the birds, the sweetness of the grass, and the feel of the wind in my mane. "Mama, I will grow up gentle as Chrome, yet strong and sure too." But most of all, we talked of how I survived the pain we both felt when we were separated so long ago, and how happy I now was. "Mama, the fear and pain grow dimmer each day, and all humans aren't like the wicked men that separated us. Oh, Mama, some humans can even learn to speak horse."

As I slept, I heard Chrome and Connella rolling in the field, and the birds singing. I felt the warm sun on my back, smelled the fresh hay next to me, and felt safe. I knew I still had much to learn. After all, I still didn't know how to blow smoke out of my nose or puff myself up to protect my family from a coyote. With a smile in my heart, I slept on.

Twenty-eight

Learning

Through darkness he's come
To light and new day
The dear little one
Who had lost his way

Shaking my head, I looked around. Chrome and Connella were no longer napping, but up enjoying some of the left over hay in the meadow. I looked at them hungrily; my heart and mind were shaken from my memories. I trotted over and hoped they were done needing space. I was sorely in need of some friends and comfort. Soon it would be supper time. Hopefully I wouldn't need to learn more about space today.

Sure enough, Marta was there. I was holding back, a bit unsure of my welcome. She was giving Chrome his snuggle before opening the door to his room. In he went to wait. Then it was Connella's turn to go into her room. Before going in, Connella turned to me and put her ears back just to make sure I knew I was last before she sauntered into her room. Marta gave her a pet on her head making sure to scratch her on her favorite place.

Finally Marta turned to me, "Come on, little one. It's time for supper now." Apparently she didn't need space just then, so before going into my room to wait for supper, I put my head down and slowly walked over to get my cuddle.

We all waited quietly. Chrome didn't even need to be scolded for jumping around in his stall, and soon all we could hear was the sound of an occasional snort.

Supper over, I waited quietly for Marta to let me out. No pushing tonight, I thought, hoping I wouldn't have any more space lessons if I continued to be extremely polite. I still wasn't really sure what space meant yet, but I thought it meant I shouldn't push Marta. Maybe Chrome would have an answer for me, I thought walking over to join him at his hay pile. I really hadn't had a good day today; it had been too full of awful memories. Hopefully tomorrow would be better.

"Chrome what does it mean that I need to learn space? Marta was very stern with me today, I'm embarrassed, and I don't like the feeling."

"But you just won't leave it be. I don't know if it's because you were taken away from your mother so young, or maybe it's because you were at the stable with only foals and humans friends.

Dinky, you have a tendency to get into people's faces, following too closely or trying to push your way to the front. Either way, sometimes you do get pushy. That's the best I can explain it. Marta and Ken will teach you more.

You still haven't learned your place. Don't get me wrong. I genuinely like you, and other than Connella, you're my best friend. So I am not the best one to teach you."

"You're my best friend. Why can't you teach me so it wouldn't be so embarrassing? You don't talk sternly to me in front of everyone."

"That's part of the problem. It's too easy for you to distract me, and we play instead. No, it must be Marta and Ken. Connella will sometimes help, and I will when I think of it. Keep in mind that in the beginning it can be a bit uncomfortable. It is hard to learn to understand all the new rules, but it's part of the process of learning to be a part of the human world. It's also a part of learning to be a horse. We must live in both worlds. Luckily Ken and Marta spend time in our world and this makes it better for all of us. Did you think about what I said earlier, Dinky?"

"Chrome, today I remembered my past like you told me I had to. It was scary for me, and some things were awful, but I think you're right. Being separated from my mother and living under so much angst made me afraid to be alone. If I'm not the center of attention, I'm afraid it will end and I'll lose my place again."

"Dinky, I'm proud of you. Today you learned more than I believed possible. You still have a long way to go, but admitting the problem is the first step. There was too much loss in your younger days. You're safe here with us, Dinky. Remember if you need to talk about the past, both Connella and I will listen and maybe we will be able to help."

"Maybe someday, Chrome. Right now I'm going to let it go for a while, try to learn from it, and be happy."

"Well, Dinky, the offer is there. We're your family. Now let's finish our supper, please."

Epilogue

Dinky will be four this spring. Since he has been with us, he has grown to nearly sixteen hands. His coat is beginning to show many white hairs, and the bottom of his tail is gold and white. He still teases Chrome and Connella unmercifully until he riles them up enough to play with him. He is seldom chased away and is seen following Chrome like a shadow, taking turns eating with Chrome and Connella, or sometimes all three eat from the same hay pile.

He's slowly learning not to nip or chew on everything, yet he still loves to try to play with the manure fork or the wheel barrow when we're trying to clean the field or the stalls. He now goes into his room nearly every meal without the need for a lead rope and is learning to walk and whoa nicely, though he's still struggling with what's expected of him in the round pen.

Sometimes he just stands and watches the back hills with a faraway look on his face, and one wonders if he is thinking of his mother, Lucky, or his early days. Then we will once again see the sparkle in his eyes, and he's our little boy again wanting cuddles, hugs and reassurance.

He will always be an imp. He's incredibly bright and always curious, especially about anything and everything that's happening around him. He has the sweetest expressions, unless he is being ornery, stubborn or trying to push a new boundary.

He's healthy, happy, and loved, and I believe he knows it. It's now only occasionally that either Chrome or Connella feel the need to reprimand him. Mostly he has settled in and understands the workings of his little herd. Sometimes you can still see the shy, timid, frightened little foal peering through his eyes and you know he is remembering.

He is nearly always first at the fence to meet someone new or to greet us when we come out to visit. He still fights a bit over his lessons, but that too is only a matter of time and work. Chrome and Connella still love and adore him. They still watch over him when he is sleeping in the meadow on a sunny afternoon or in his stall at night if they hear or see something that worries them. I believe he will always be their little brother, and he is growing up to be a strong, sweet tempered, and beautiful young horse.

Ken and I have had little contact with his old stable, though they did attempt at one point to force me to provide pictures of him each year along with his medical, worming, and shoeing records. Going so far as